Miss You, PAT

Miss You, PAT

Collected Memories of
NY's Bravest of the Brave,
Captain Patrick J. Brown

By SHARON WATTS

Book and Cover Design, and Cover Art: Kathleen Massaro

Cover Photo credits:
Fire Rescue, 1991 – Pulitzer Nominated Photo published by the *New York Post*
© Courtesy of the Estate of Michael Norcia

Cover Photo: © Joshua Paul

Back Cover Photo: © James Keyser

ISBN 978-1-4303-2704-2

Library of Congress Control Number 2007907227

Published by Lulu.com

AUTHOR'S NOTE

Time heals all wounds, the saying goes, gentrifying experiences as varied as fingerprints. Threads of memory of love mesh with razor ribbons of loss. Mismatched knitting needles somehow begin to do their work, making a patch that never quite exactly fits the hole.

This project took on a life of its own from the very beginning. It was always to be about Captain Patrick J. Brown—one of the greatest legends in the history of the New York City Fire Department. But because Pat was a seeker, a man struggling with his humanity while forging his own spiritual path, the stories acquired other dimensions that reflected not only Pat's search, but also his influence on those whose paths he crossed.

Pat Brown "belonged" to everyone. That feeling, or rather that fact, became evident as I collected people's remembrances of him. Pat's story is infused with the stories of the individuals who shared theirs with me.

Not at all a conventional narrative, this story offers itself up in patchwork blocks of anecdotes, information, reminiscences, points of view, moods. I tried to keep the connecting stitches smooth and even, each loop one of love, admiration, gratitude, fortitude.

I hope that the final result not only honors Patrick J. Brown but also conveys the organic process of healing that came part and parcel with the honor of knowing and loving him.

Nothing about Pat was conventional. Or easy. But he definitely was memorable.

PATRICK J. BROWN

I go into those deep and dark places.
I am a man of anger, but under the anger is sadness,
and under the sadness is unconditional love,
and under the unconditional love is innocence.

PROLOGUE: December 2002

The tribute walls at Grand Central have come down. They were in the Lexington Passage, originally set up as information posts, but they quickly turned to message boards to communicate with and mourn the missing, the dead. A pink poster of construction paper with a picture of Pat was posted sometime in early 2002. I first saw it in February. Over the course of the year, it became a sort of conceptual crazy quilt for notes from people Pat had left behind. As it evolved, it confirmed what the heading said:

NYC LOVES PAT BROWN.

Pat touched so many people in so many walks of life. Yoga practitioners left blessings and affirmations of his inspiring their practice, and someone added a Xerox of Pat from *Yoga Journal,* personalized with an "Om Shanti." His fellow karate-ka added their "Osu Sensei"s, because for many years he trained with and inspired them as well. Messages were posted from brother firefighters, a myriad of friends, childhood sweethearts, blood relations, former neighbors from growing up in Queens and current ones from Manhattan's Stuyvesant Town, people who were recipients of his charity, and others, like me, who, in spite of being very close to him, had no idea just how beloved he was or how far his influence extended.

I visited the Grand Central tribute every time I was in the station. It was part of my routine, and I took comfort in it. I saw it evolve and wondered if others who added to it also witnessed its blossoming into an amazing piece of memorial art. How fragile it was. One day it would be gone. One day it was. A replacement poster went up, with the remnant of the pink paper still tacked to the top of the wall. The note from the maker claimed that someone loved Pat so much that she or he took the original tribute. Was this a chastisement or simply an acknowledgment? I read it as a reprimand, feeling as if something cherished had been stolen. But then again, I knew that one day I would come out of the train and see that the whole tribute wall was down. And that happened also.

We all have memorial walls and tribute posters in our hearts for anyone we love who dies. And no vandal or clean-up crew can take them down.

"Life is a journey, and love is what makes that journey worthwhile."

—UNKNOWN

Journal Entry — May 28, 2003

Three days ago, I turned fifty and was given a travel journal by a friend of Pat whom I never knew existed until a year ago. When I was still a teenager and attending art school in my new home, New York City, their paths crossed in a night of fate and violence and rescue. Her life was changed forever. Perhaps his, too. He delivered the gift of safety to a frightened, traumatized girl my own age.

Throughout the years he continued to give gifts, many times lifesaving ones. And now Pat keeps on giving to all those he left behind on 9/11. We are discovering one another, and links are forming, forged by the love we share for an amazingly unique man. The connections are healing us, with stitches weaving not only through the tears in our hearts, but patching us together as a quilt, with comfort and strength as we resume our lives.

I am on Metro-North, riding into my city. A sadness settles over me like mosquito netting as I walk the streets. Memories buzz around, always finding holes to get through—a bench where we once sat and planned our future, a coffee shop where we had a quarrel, a corner where we'd meet to decide what to eat, sushi or sushi? It was Pat's city. It was my city. And my city is gone.

Journal Entry – September 21, 2001

I have nothing written on September 11, 2001. Had I kept a journal of that day, I would have written on the train. Had it been a normal day.

I saw the first plane hit the tower as I was turning off *The Today Show* to drive the short ride down Route 9-D to Cold Spring where I planned to park and train it into Manhattan to vote. I was still registered as a city resident, having only just bought my first home the previous November. I had spent the summer fixing it up, gardening, acclimating to my new town, my new life. I was on hiatus from Pat Brown. By then I knew the routine, the pulling close and then distancing in our dance of intimacy, which had been going on for six years. But toward the summer's end, we reconnected with a long phone conversation, and when I asked if he wanted to hook up for dinner Tuesday night, September 11th, he said he couldn't. He had to work.

On the car ride to the station, the radio played music, soft rock, and I wondered if I had hallucinated the unbelievable news. The film footage on the TV was amateurish, and the newscaster sounded doubtful rather than incredulous. But then came the interruption on the radio, with the announcement that a second plane had struck the other tower, and a third had hit the Pentagon, and I was continuing on automatic pilot with the errands of that day programmed into my agenda even as I heard reports of as many as eight planes in the skies, en route to their respective targets. What was I thinking? I have no idea.

On that impossibly clear and gorgeous morning, I waited with the few others taking the off-peak 9:27. No one seemed to be aware of what was happening. Until a cabbie drove up, dispensed a commuter, and idled with his radio turned up loud for us all to hear. Regardless, like dumb sheep, we boarded the train as it rolled into the station. The conductor announced the incident, though I don't remember if he called it an attack. He had no instructions not to continue to Grand Central Terminal, and the autopilot that had assumed control of my body was still propelling me toward the city.

Ten minutes later, I was thinking of terrorism, of being caught in Manhattan with no way to return home, and of Pat rushing to the scene. Because, of course, Pat would be one of the first to respond, whether or not he was working that day. (I didn't know for a fact that he was; I only knew that he was working that night. But he would be there.) What I was *not* thinking was that the World Trade towers would collapse. That my world would be razed.

I came, somewhat, to my senses at Peekskill and abruptly exited and waited with excruciation for the next train to take me right back to where I started. Within minutes, I was headed back to my car. My Subaru pushed seventy miles per hour on the winding, sun-dappled road, racing toward a fate that was still unknowable. I entered the door and ran to the TV set and turned it on to see the beginning of the North Tower's collapse. A cosmic shudder sent its shock waves to the core of me. I made a frantic and emotional call to Pat's apartment and left a message that I had just seen the second tower collapse and knew he was down there. A short while later, I made another call, saying with impossible calm that I knew he was okay and to *please*, please call me and confirm my utter faith in this knowledge. I curled up into the fetal position on the sofa and stayed there the rest of the day. I knew nothing definitively, yet I knew all.

MIKE DALY – *New York Daily News* – September 12, 2001

Retired Firefighter Kevin Horan, now fire safety director at the World Trade Center, came up with his head bandaged and his arm in a sling.

"I just saw pieces of bodies," he said.

Horan set off in search of his old unit, Ladder 3. You knew two of the company, and the day held no more beautiful sight than one of them standing unhurt on Liberty St. Your heart sank when he told you the other man had been on the 50th floor when the tower went down. You again looked at the rubble and remembered when you last saw your friend, the two of you laughing and joking as you marched to a communion breakfast.

E-mail to **MIKE DALY**

Subject: PAT BROWN???????????????????

Date: September 12, 2001 3:40:07 p.m., Eastern Daylight Time

Dear Mike—I met you at dinner in 1996 when I was engaged to be married to
Pat Brown. I need to know—was that who you were referring to on the fiftieth
floor, from Ladder 3, that didn't make it? Please, let me know what you know.

Journal Entry – September 21, 2001, *continued*

After the long day of walking, walking through the strange streets of this
new world, I was emotionally and physically beat, but not ready to throw
in the crumpled towel. I doubted that I could make it through the entire
6:00 p.m. yoga class at Jivamukti, Pat's haven these past few years. I had
to be put on the waiting list for the fully reserved class—after-work stress
had been replaced with some awful mutant variation.

I once asked Pat as we compared our yoga schools (mine in Brooklyn)
who his favorite teacher was. He said, "Kristin."

I dragged myself to class with heavy heart and swollen feet. The laven-
der and turquoise room was full, with quiet apprehension filling every
chakra, and Barbara was the instructor. She had us assume a pose lying
flat, with arms stretched over our heads and backs arched over rolled-up
blankets, our hearts exposed to the universe. Speaking gently about the
terror and loss we all experienced, she mentioned Pat by name. Tears that
had brimmed up to the surface of my closed eyes the moment the chanting began now spilled down my temples and into my ears—silent sobs
that could no longer be contained by any yogic breath. Someone grabbed
my hands, holding me tight through the length of the pose, meeting my
pain and making it hers to bear with me. I didn't know until our fingers
let go that it was Kristin. She only knew me as someone who needed her
at that moment.

Missing Pat in the physical sense is almost unbearable. I can no longer touch his silky salt-and-pepper hair, or smell the salty perfume of sweat on his chest, his throat. But I can begin to feel his presence, and it is a revelation. Indescribable. Pat had guided Kristin to comfort me.

KRISTIN LEIGH & DAVID KLEIN — *New Life Magazine* — December, 2001

Pat always wore an FDNY shirt when he took class. Students would tell me that they had seen him on the nightly news, or on a fire truck (in the front seat, next to the driver) racing through the streets, sirens blaring. One of my fellow teachers told me of hearing her name called out by Pat over the fire truck's loudspeaker as it drove by. One evening, he showed my friends and me around the Ladder 3 stationhouse. There was something sweet about the sight of Pat's yoga mat, hung up to dry on top of his locker.

Pat, a tough-but-sweet man of few words, was a hardworking, humble yoga student who could be counted on to be in his usual spot in the classroom. While some of us knew that Pat was a firefighter, we didn't truly understand the extent of his heroism. He never let on that he was one of the department's most decorated men, that he was a true legend to his fellow firefighters. He never spoke of his personal accomplishments. In the course of the two years in which he was a student at the Jivamukti Center, more and more people got to know him, if only for a smile and a wave and a word of greeting. We always felt good knowing he was there; we had a fireman in our studio, and it made us feel safe.

At the end of his first class, a teacher and former firefighter came over and asked me, "Do you know who that is? That's Pat Brown. He's a real hero."

From that day on, Pat came to class three, four, five times a week, as often as his schedule allowed. His passion was unmistakable. Sometimes he took a morning class after working an all-night shift, and then he would jog home afterward.

Pat gave it his all. He was always focused and enthusiastic. Students often come out of difficult poses before the teacher says to; Pat never did. He stayed with each pose until the end and was always fully engaged in the practice. Pat knew the value of discipline, and that is one reason he loved yoga so much—because it demands both compassion and a deep, even rigorous, commitment. It helped him in many ways. Once, the day after some firefighters were killed in Queens, I noticed that Pat was shaking during final relaxation, trying to hold back tears. Afterward I sat with him... he told us how hard it was to accept the loss of his friends, guys he had known for such a long time. Yoga helped him to work through some of his grief that day.

A few months later, September 11th happened. For many of us, it was Pat whom we thought of when we went down a mental checklist. That night, with the city ghostly quiet and the air still acrid with the smell of the blasts, I went over to his stationhouse and learned that Pat, along with 11 of the 27 men in his squad, had been lost in the tower collapse. In the days that followed, hope faded, and we had to grapple with the enormity and finality of the devastation.

Numbness, shock, and sadness made it difficult to focus on anything, let alone taking a yoga class, or teaching one. Yet it was a comfort being in Brahma, the big room at the Center. It was the place I associated with Pat. Looking for him to be in his usual place, and realizing he wasn't coming back, filled me with sadness.

As more and more students learned about the loss of our friend, there was a great outpouring of emotion. The sounds of weeping could be heard during chanting at the beginning and end of class, and grief for Pat filled up the same room where, months ago, Pat had grieved for his fallen brothers.

Someone set up a bulletin board, and many people wrote heartfelt messages. One person wrote: "And you admired MY practice?"

Another wrote, "Pat, thanks for the example you set, and thanks for lending me the shorts that day."

We wonder how we can carry on his legacy of bravery, selfless service, and compassion. Most of us will never be heroic in the sense that Pat was, but we want to honor his memory. We want to behave in ways that would make Pat happy, not give in to despair, distrust, or cynicism. Pat would want us to live our lives.

In Union Square, which in the weeks after September 11th became a massive shrine and memorial, I saw a sign that felt very apt. It said, "When the pain wears away, please don't forget." I will not. I was Pat's teacher; now Pat has become mine. He was a living example of true devotion. He embodied the ideal of selfless service—every day of his life—by putting others first, by facing down his fears, by being so brave.

Pat is free now. I can imagine him watching us right now. And I bet he's wondering why we're making such a fuss over him.

PAT BROWN — *Yoga Journal* — December, 2001 (excerpt from an interview conducted in the summer of 2001)

"In my job, we have no warm-up," says Pat Brown, a captain with Ladder Company 3 in the New York City Fire Department. "We just put on 100 pounds of equipment, run in, climb up ladders, and crash through windows. I love yoga because it's hard and because my practice has really helped me emotionally and spiritually.

"I've been through a lot of really bad things in the fire department," he says. "There's a tremendous amount of guilt and trauma. I work through my emotions while I'm doing asanas. Breathing and feeling all of these feelings doesn't make it easier. It's just different than dealing with the feelings in other ways. The pain is more incisive and deep, but it's not flying around. It's just as sad, but it's clean."

Journal Entry

Not long after 9/11, I found myself slowly unfurling from my fetal position, both physically and mentally. I would sit in front of my computer screen and trawl cyberspace like a wounded shark, devouring anything that related to my loss. "Googling" Captain Pat Brown became a ritual—the equivalent of morning meditation and vitamins and coffee and reading the newspaper, all rolled into one. I needed to click on every link. I found paths that were as diverse as those of a maze, yet they all led to Pat. Some links were to the media, some to various personal Web Sites, and some to tribute sites established to honor each of the heroes and victims.

I found childhood friends, like his old sweetheart Liz, and his Explorer Scout buddy Joe, now wearing a "Bracelet for America" with Pat's name, fighting fires in Colorado. Congressional hearings cited Pat's final heroic efforts, refusing to abandon "forty severely burnt people" in Tower One. There were reports from fellow firefighters on the scene, who witnessed "the gallant Captain Brown," as Mike Daly of the *Daily News* christened him, dashing up the stairs for the final time. There were tributes left by strangers who had seen him on TV or read about him and knew an exceptional person had been taken from us. And there were messages from acquaintances, family, and so many friends. The personal outpourings of people whose lives had been touched by Pat were a revelation. I had had no idea how he impacted those whose paths he crossed. I only knew how he impacted me…

"Tears are like rain. They loosen up our soil so we can grow in different directions."

—Virginia Casey

Journal Entry — March 29, 2002

More than six months have passed since 9/11. Spring is here, sort of— in reality, and even a little bit in my heart. Contentment incongruously laced with a deep sadness is what I find while doing yard work, shuffling through Benjamin Moore paint chips, illustrating a children's book. I guess that is the best I can hope for, settling into my second year of home ownership, balancing the burden of debt with the rewards of building a nest.

Books documenting 9/11 are now coming out, like Dennis Smith's *Report From Ground Zero*, which I devoured. I need to know—who saw Pat, when, where, what he said, what he was doing. The book viscerally wrenched my heart with its personal eyewitness accounts from people at Ground Zero, an unfathomable POV.

I stumbled across a new memorial in the Union Square subway station. All the victims' names are posted on large sheets of paper attached to the tiled wall. A laminated mass card is taped next to Pat's name, and the now ubiquitous personal messages written to him. "You had the smile of an Angel." "Miss You." Again I am reminded that I had no awareness when he was alive of how many people he touched, how many people knew and loved him.

DENNIS SMITH – Excerpt from *Report From Ground Zero*

...and Brown. Brown. Paddy Brown. It is especially hard for me to
come to grips with the passing of Paddy, the fireman's fireman, the
object of affection of all who knew him, men and women. ...Paddy
had a chestful of medals and he wore a modest heart. There would
be no lasting pages of history in our department without men like
(him). And now Paddy won't be there any longer, first due at a fire
and first to arrive at a burning door. It is as if Park Avenue had been
lifted right out of the city, and though you could still travel uptown
and downtown, the trip wouldn't be as memorable without it. Our
future fires will be fought by good men, but somehow it won't be
the same without Paddy.

Journal Entry – April 11, 2002

I had coffee with Dennis Smith today on Madison Avenue. He is not interested in writing a book about Pat, though he thinks there is an audience
for one. He confirms my belief that a collection of stories about Paddy
Brown, the "gallant Captain Brown," the charismatic FDNY legend,
should be collected and published for all to know and remember before
the stories are gone and forgotten or never known at all.

And what about some of the others? The ones Pat shared with so many
of us, individually? A passage I read in a book reverberated and I recalled
those intimacies...

Sue Monk Kidd – *The Secret Life of Bees*

"I watched him, filled with tenderness and ache, wondering what
it was that connected us. Was it the wounded places down inside
people that sought each other out, that bred a kind of love between
them?...

"I'll write all this down for you," I said. "I'll put it in a story."
...It's something everybody wants—for someone to see the hurt
done to them and set it down like it matters."

Journal Entry – June 5, 2003

I have started a project. It involves collecting stories from people about Pat. Stories of how, in large or small ways, he changed their lives. Stories about his rescues as a legend in the FDNY. I have tried for a couple years now to find someone to do this, considering and approaching several established authors, biographers, and journalists, but with no luck. Then, coincidentally, it was suggested I do a collaborative effort with a woman writer who met Pat a week before 9/11, because in that brief meeting, he changed *her* life. A work conflict caused her to bow out, and I am left holding the reins. My desire that this be done for Pat is overriding my apprehension. With all the coincidences reformatting my thought patterns, I am starting to feel that Pat has guided this back into my lap, and so that gives me strength to add to my conviction.

SANDI BACHOM

I met Captain Patty Brown of the FDNY on September 4, 2001. Although I met him only once, my life was transformed by the meeting. As are, I have found, all the lives that Pat seamlessly walked through. His angelic presence changed us all. It was as if he illuminated and revealed our true selves to us. The thing that I took away from that first meeting and will always keep in my heart was Pat's grace and humility. All I can share is my experience and the stories of those I have met since September 11, people who knew him far better than I. He has inspired me, as he has and will continue to inspire those who called him Son, Brother, Friend or Captain...

"The Captain is the reason I'm here," a brazenly bald Brendan declares with a brogue as thick as Irish stew.

"How so?" I ask, pondering his shiny dome. (Genetics? Or self-inflicted blade?)

"I ride my bike here every day from the Bronx, and the Captain says to me, 'Don't you have a helmet?' and I say 'No.' One day, I came in, and he'd bought me one." His sad blue eyes, piercing, lock mine with astonishing loyalty and love.

Clinging to the once-majestic frames, like some filigree lace, the shredded steel, defying gravity. Scrawled on a great white sheet, a giant Post-It to a missing brother: "R.I.P Capt. Patty Brown." It was on CNN. I make these tapes and take them to the guys. Any excuse to see them. The Mikes, Jim Wind, Tim, Gonzo, Brendan. And in return for these mementos, a big bear hug. And I know I'm getting the better end of the deal.

A week to the day before this all happened, I was having dinner with my friend James R. and Pat. This was my first meeting with the unassuming man, of whom it later would be said that he was a "hero of mythic proportions."

Startlingly handsome. Movie star handsome. "Like Charles Bronson," the boys in Ladder 3 insist, or Harrison Ford to my eye. Soft-spoken with a gentle humility and sweetness, a quiet oxymoron contradicting his credentials. Vietnam veteran. Firefighter. Who could not get through the evening without acknowledging, with trembling voice, the loss that day of a young "brother," because each and every loss to this band of brothers is like some collective amputation.

This poet warrior, speaking so honestly of this pain: "I'd like to quote Schumann," he smiles slyly, "the composer.

'When I tried to write a song about Love, I wrote a song about Pain. When I tried to write a song about Pain, I wrote a song about Love.'" A silent reverence fell on the room.

It is October 9th, John Lennon's birthday. Hundreds of us are crowded into The Bowery Ballroom to hear our favorite cover band, the Fab Faux. And if you close your eyes, you can hear John plucking out the first notes to "Imagine" on the piano. A hush and sadness blanket the room. The tears just flow, shamelessly, in public, as they have so many times since this thing happened; it is the same for all of us. There is no having to explain why my cheeks are wet, because we *all* know why. But now, the words have an extra meaning, as is the case with great art. It becomes deeper, an anthem. As if perfectly written for just this moment, and such was the case with this song.

As the last chord is played, Will Lee, in his "Our Man in Havana" white suit framed against an American flag, leans into the mike and sweetly, softly, with great reverence, says: "That song is for everyone in this room. For everyone you ever loved, or even hated. And for all the Patty Browns. I wonder what John would have thought of all this?"

I go by Ladder 3 every day now. I joke with the guys; they are so eager to laugh. They have lost twelve of twenty-seven of their brothers, and they are still eager to laugh. There is great healing in laughter. I have always known this, but God has given me a direct experience. I have believed for a long time that if we can find humor in a thing, we have already begun to heal. That laughter is the physical manifestation of this—the sound effect of healing. I have learned this from the firefighters of Ladder 3. They, who have the least reason to laugh, are the first to make a joke, and everyone laughs just a little louder than usual.

Last night, James and I and some other friends of Pat went back to The Adriatic where I met Pat for the first time. James ordered "a *big* salad," making a wide gesture with his hands. "Pasta with marinara." And something about olives. He really drew out the order and was smiling the whole time. All the while, Pat's favorite Russian waitress was laughing, but she didn't write any of it down, and then I got it. It was Pat's regular order. It was what he always ordered there on Tuesday nights. It was so sweet and loving. We lifted a glass of Diet Coke. We laughed and shared stories of heroism and, above all, friendship. The type that few of us are privileged to know even once in our lifetimes.

Journal Entry – May 1, 2002

Today was one of those rare, good, full days in the city—very satisfying in unexpected ways, and very much needed. The weather was glorious, arcing from cool to warm under sunny skies—a Post-It on my brain to clean and organize my closets soon.

First stop was Pat's tribute at Grand Central. I really expected it to be down; the yoga pages that had been attached had fallen off, gotten trampled and swept away. But there were a few more new notes, and after paying my respects, I was off and running to a day full of appointments. On my way to the bank, my heart gave a little lurch—the Ladder 3 truck was parked on lower 5th Avenue—only Pat was no longer in the front passenger seat. But I did see Jim Wind, the lieutenant and occasionally Pat's chauffeur. What a sweetie—always with his raspy muffler of a voice and his big welcome hug. I told him Kristin was opening a new yoga studio a couple blocks from the firehouse and then dashed off to another errand when who do I see but Kristin! As if Pat were pulling all the right strings for me to have a good day—to feel his presence more than his absence. To miss him, but to also enjoy my time in his old neighborhood. To resume my life.

Journal Entry – June 16, 2002

I am simply not motivated in any direction these days. Why is that? A delayed realization that life truly, finally, is not as it was? A deep hole fills me, where once lived the knowledge that Pat was available to me in tangible form. (Or not, depending on his mood.)

Only in the garden do I have any real sense of purpose or peace. Ironically, I never owned more than a single stoic philodendron in all my thirty years of apartment living. Less than ever are money and "success" motivating factors for me. In a strange way, I feel as if I am tilling the soil that will nourish me the second half of my life. I am hitting submerged rocks, but a rocky path still feels like the right path, and my clearing it seems to be part of the plan.

"Kites rise highest against the wind——not with it."

—— Winston Churchill

Journal Entry – December 12, 2003

Today, for the first time since 2001, I was in the elevator of 319 Avenue C. The doors closed; the dark green enamel walls surrounded me, and the memory of riding up with Pat formed an eerily comforting shroud. Pat—— with his playful grabbing, or shuffling through his mail, or just holding the plastic bag with its sole content: a pint of ice cream in pre-yoga years, a pint of frozen yogurt after his nutritional enlightenment. Most likely we would have been returning from a dinner in the neighborhood, always by cab. (Pat might have run or biked from Brooklyn to Manhattan or from Stuyvesant Town to Harlem, but from dinner to après dinner, it was strictly on the meter.)

I vividly remember the ascent to Apartment 11-A, fueled by the anticipation of entering the routine of being with Pat at home. Home was a "1BR RIV VU" with fire engine red carpeting, a baby grand piano, a Mickey Mouse telephone, a black leather couch, and the FDNY work calendar open on the table revealing his myriad appointments. (It also served as his athletic diary, with running times and places logged in and karate classes attended, the comfort of all his routines laid out in cryptic scratches of his pen.) The towels, running shorts, FDNY T-shirts, and karate gear were draped, drying, over the shower-curtain rod, chair backs, the sofa, and the bicycle leaning against the baby grand. Inspirational books lay strewn about, open with their spines facing the heavens, so that at any given moment he could resume *The Road Less Traveled* or some other guide to inner peace.

And so, the memories that washed over me like a tsunami did a quick ebbing as I exited on the fifth floor, not eleventh. And I waited for Ingrid Morales, a medical technician from the Philippines, and her story of how Pat came into her life.

INGRID MORALES

When they brought me home, it was the beginning of when Patrick touched my life. Because before the accident, we just say, "Hi" and "Hello." I got two jobs, he got how many jobs, who knows, you know, we just see each other, casual thing, say hello, maybe, "How are you?" "Have a good day," you know, things like that. But I came in, and he was right there near the elevator; he holds the door and said, "What happened to you?!"

And I said, "Oh, a truck, it hit me." And he said, "That's really bad!" And I say, "Yes," and I have my neck brace, my back brace, my knee brace, and I was arguing with my nephew (that I would be okay), and Patrick was listening to this conversation and said, "You really want to go home now."

I said, "Home is home."

So one day I'm going out slowly, and I was kicking my little bag of laundry, and Patrick saw me and said, "Oh boy! I thought I was hard-headed! I didn't know there was somebody worse than me!"

I said, "Shhh!" and I was kicking it slowly. So he picked it up and put it in the laundry room, and he said, "Do you need help when you want to pick it up?" And I said, "Patrick, it's just a few pieces."

"Okay! Okay! " and he laughs, and he left me.

And the next time he saw me pushing a small cart, my Rolls Royce I call it, I still had my vertigo. I'm holding whatever in one arm and pushing, that's also my exercise, and Pat just grabbed my cart and said, "Oh yeah? Oh yeah?" And he shook his head, and he pushed the cart to my door. Sometimes he'd see me going out early in the morning: "Where you going now?"

I said, "To my therapy."

"Oh, good news—someone's having therapy!" and he would just keep jogging.

So, he became a part of my life and part of my healing. You know, you feel strong... I'm by myself in here; my family is in Queens, in Jersey—you feel secure. You know somebody's there on the 11th floor, as he said, "Anytime you need help, don't hesitate to call me upstairs."

I didn't know what his work is, I didn't even know his last name is Brown, I just know him as Pat.

The last time I saw him before September 11th, he was in his dress uniform. When I came in from therapy and opened the door, he was standing there ready to go out, and I said, "Oh my god! I did not know you were such a good-looking kid! Could I knock on your door?"

And he said, "Uh-oh!" (laughing). And that was it.

I put one of his pictures on my altar. I tell my nieces and nephews never to forget this day. I put it there with Jesus, and I think he'd appreciate that; he's with the angels. Every time before I close the door, I say a prayer, and I say, "Patrick, watch our house and the building, okay?" You know, I tell everybody: "Don't forget."

NASSER HASHASH — Stuyvesant Town Deli-owner

Every time I'd see him, he was always sweating and running and jogging. I knew Pat, to tell you the truth, just as a customer in the neighborhood, on a first name basis—Patty or Pat—and he used to come to the store practically every day, and he'd buy his coffee or his Diet Coke, and he'd say, "Hi, how are you?" And you wouldn't think from his modesty that he was such a legendary guy in the Fire Department, or New York in general. I found out from reading all the stories after he died. I never knew—he never talked about all those bravery things you read about, and I guess that's what makes him special, and that's why a lot of people take a liking to him, because he's very modest. A nice, quiet guy, and he dedicated practically all his life to simplicity. Pat would never say, "I did this, I did that," always keeps it to himself.

One of the things that strikes me about Pat is that all those things he did in his life—how come so many people never knew? I don't think he cared so much for the recognition because that's the way he believes, that he was born to do those things.

ROSEMARY McKENNA — Resident of Stuyvesant Town

Pat was my neighbor. A quiet guy who always smiled and said hello on the elevator. And if anyone knows a Manhattan apartment building, that was a lot to get from a neighbor. Before 9/11, I'm not sure how many people in the building knew about his legendary reputation as a fireman; I know that I didn't. He was just "the friendly fireman from 11" to us—the guy who helped a neighbor who was recuperating from a bad car accident, got someone's car started, gave someone a ride to work, or gave a kid a boost to push the elevator button. Since then, we've learned that his good deeds around Stuyvesant Town were nothing compared to what he did in his life.

Journal Entry — January 5, 2004

"No good deed goes unpunished."

I woke up today with, if not a New Year's resolution, at least a fresh resolve to apply myself more rigorously to the Pat Project. Unfortunately, a sucker punch landed before I even had my first cup of coffee. It came in the form of an e-mail from a man who knew Pat from the job and was his friend as well, laying into me about just how unsupportive he is toward my book, accusing me of using him as a "key in the door." This simply is not true. But how many men in the fire department has he possibly turned against me? What damage control, if any, can I muster? I can't allow myself to give him or anyone the emotional power over me to derail my beliefs. I can't give up.

But it also makes me delve deeper into the phenomenon of Pat's ability to cause so many people of both sexes to be so intensely protective/possessive of him. (And what exactly is that fine line of a slash between those two words?)

The sender of this e-mail has no rational reason to be so vehemently against me, personally. He knew I was in Pat's life over the years; we never had any friction, nor did we bond. I know that there is a backlash because of the damage caused by a previous work of fiction based on Pat's life, written by a former lover and published just following the events of 9/11. The portrayals and betrayals in that book ignited the same anger, the same protective instincts in Pat's friends as they did in me. Yet, I think there's more.

Pat was so able to tap into people's pain, so empathetic to our hurt, our shame, our weakness and self-doubts, that he made us feel emotionally safe. He made it all okay; he gave a nudge to our backs, letting us know we were not alone. And iron-strong bonds of trust and loyalty were formed. Maybe for the ones whose hurt runs so deep and with currents so strong, Pat, after 9/11, became an iconic presence that nurtures a type of righteous possessiveness toward him. Those roots have taken hold, tangled and forced into a confinement of spiritual space, allowing no room for healthy growth.

PETE BONDY – Rescue 2 FDNY, Retired
I couldn't imagine Patty Brown married. He belonged to everybody. Nobody owned him. He had too many people to take care of.

SIMONE ZAPPA – Pat's Friend and Neighbor
Oh, Patty… I mean, trying to explain Patty… I never called him Pat. Never. I used to ask him: "Paddy? Two D's? Patty?" He didn't care. He didn't know! So I used to call him Patty, with two T's.

When I met Patty (in the 70s), he was definitely a "party boy." Well, we were very young. I was very young! He wasn't that young! (Laughter). We had a thing on and off for a couple of years, but then we just became really good friends.

What was so amazing about him was he was always there. Now, I always knew he would be there if I needed anything. When I got my divorce, Patty was the one I called. When he hurt himself, I would be the one *he* called. We always had that type of friendship, but I was always so amazed——I had a big fight with my boyfriend and I quit my job and I'd head home and I'd be sobbing and who would I run into on the street—— Patty. Or I'd be on my rollerblades and I would fall, and who would out of the blue be there to pick me up——Patty. Or some guys would be giving me a hard time, and all of a sudden, Patty would appear, and I'd say, *"Where do you come from?"* And it would always be, and so he was like a guardian angel. Besides knowing I could always bother him, he was always there for me.

Patty and I go way back. I consider myself one of his dearest friends, though we didn't see each other that often. But when he died, all these people surfaced who were good friends of Pat, and especially all these women, and my biggest fear was that I wouldn't get into his funeral. I mean, nobody *knew* me. And I'd known Patty for twenty-two years! I never tried to say I was his girlfriend, I never tried to say I loved him. Patty taught me to drink my first shot of tequila. People accepted that.

He was such a little boy. The phone would ring, and I'd pick it up, and that voice! "Simona-san! Look out your window." And I look out my window. "Hey there!" he'd wave from the payphone on the corner. That's what I loved the most about him; he was such a brave, serious man, but at the same time, he could be so silly and fun.

But also, he was dark. Dark. *Dark.* Vietnam——very heavy on him. That's when he was the crazy fireman, doing all the crazy things. The Disco Era. I do think Patty and I had a special bond. I really truly believe that back in the day, if Patty could have married anybody, he would have married me. I don't think it would have worked! He used to call me up back then, like four or five in the morning, and he'd be in a club somewhere. "Simone, you know I really love you. I'm just too fucked-up to tell you." I got so many of those, and I actually told him that recently, and he goes, "Yeah, yeah, yeah." He goes, "I can't be with anybody." Which was such a sad thing, because he hated to be alone.

After 9/11 his sister-in-law told me he had come to some sort of peace with himself. He called me just before that day and wanted to come over. I don't think he was calling me to say "You're the one," though I do think Patty did love me. It was many years too late for that. I hope he was calling me to say, "I found peace, finally."

Journal Entry – January 13, 2004

I must remember the fact that my Pat Project is a labor of love, not a battle of wills. Ironically, this love we all have for Pat seems to erupt at times into turf wars, and so my agenda is not necessarily common ground for healing and honoring.

Surprisingly, the easier part is the cold calling, with the harder part being the inevitable follow-up. Sometimes I feel fragile and tentative, lacking in both charisma and confidence to inspire. Diametrically opposed to Pat's attributes. Although we both are shy people at the core, our balancing dynamism exhibits itself in different ways. Pat's men would rally behind him anytime, anywhere, unquestioning, up the stairs, into the fire.

Pat, soon after I met him, tapped into the void of my personal history. My rote description of how my father was electrocuted on a utility pole when I was four reflected the general handling of loss and trauma in our family. It was absorbed quickly and swept under the rug, and any natural evolution of grief was stifled by the mores of the Eisenhower Era, or perhaps the stiff upper lip of my grandfather, who simply stopped talking about his son. Of course, my mother, my younger sister, and I made trips to the cemetery. We filled the vase and for a few moments arranged on the gravesite hyacinths at Easter, poinsettia at Christmas, and mums in autumn on the October anniversary of his death. I was just doing what was expected, like a good girl. I didn't understand what it was all about, why exactly this was how we remembered Daddy.

But Pat made me feel the loss. And he made me feel safe. He put me on a pedestal like my father had done, reminding me of the love and adulation that was snatched away at the very age that any four-year-old is quite naturally "Daddy's Girl."

Pat told me that energy does not die, and that my father's loving spirit was also in him, Pat. He made a forty-three-year-old agnostic *believe*, by giving me the keystone that would support my own evolving spiritual path. The road he had to travel in his own life to get to that place where he could shine a light on mine had to have been treacherous and difficult beyond my imagination. And he had a need to share it with me, and with others.

Train ride home...

I picked up theatre tickets on West 45th Street, a street full of memories. Times Square may have changed and "Disneyfied" beyond all recognition, but there are pockets one can stumble upon that open right up into 1972. Back then, I was as mesmerized by the Broadway theatre scene as any wannabe in a chorus line. Never mind that I was a nineteen-year-old art major; my heart led me to waitress first and then live in the area whose streets were "paved with gold" and walked by prostitutes and other denizens of the night. I remember the Camelot, a post-war nondescript elevator apartment building on the corner of 8th Avenue, whose Gilded Grape transvestite bar spilled garish outcasts from normal society onto the sidewalks and into the backseats of cars cruising for the type of action that Hell's Kitchen was known for in those pre-Giuliani years.

I would leave my waitress job, still wearing the brown-and-white gingham-checked apron, and make my way home at 2:00 a.m. One of those trips resulted in my being grabbed from behind with my arm twisted back, and pushed into my tenement's dark hallway. The subsequent rape, trial, and the numbing effect that resulted were viewed by me as an unfortunate rite of passage toward being a survivor in New York City. I would mention it casually, perhaps too casually, in early conversations with men that I met. Not one ever had the reaction that I didn't even know I was looking for. Until Pat Brown. Pat could empathize because he had gone through his own hell. Pat could supply the anger and retroactive protection that I was too stubborn and numb and dumb to know that I even needed all those years ago. Pat tapped into the pain (still submerged in a pool of emotional stagnation), threw his coat down, and offered himself to me as an escort out. We shared our memories of the squalor as well as the fun of Times Square in the early 70s, with a perverse pride that we not only survived but overcame. We compared our battle scars as we basked in the safety and comfort of having found each other.

"The child is father to the man."   ——Gerard Manley Hopkins

Journal Entry – January 18, 2004

I turned on my computer yesterday to see a solitary e-mail with the subject head "Re: Pat Brown." I didn't immediately recognize the e-mail address as that of Captain John Vigiano, whom I had sort of shot an arrow in the air toward, during the holidays. John was Pat's lieutenant at Rescue 2, and I had been hesitant in contacting him because he had lost two sons in the World Trade Center. I didn't want to infringe on his privacy, yet I sensed in him a grave decency and dignity and kindness from the film clips and articles I had seen and read. I hoped that he would have the inclination to help me honor Pat, despite or because of his own unfathomable loss.

JOHN VIGIANO – Captain FDNY, Retired

I met Pat at the Rock (the term used to describe the training academy). There was some sort of ceremony, and he was sitting near me in the auditorium. Somehow the conversation got around to the Marine Corps, and that began the friendship. I, too, was a former Marine, but unlike Pat, never served in combat. As the conversation progressed, I asked why he was still working in Manhattan—the work was in Brooklyn, and Rescue 2 was the *only* place to work. Well, in a few months, Pat transferred to Rescue 2.

While in Manhattan, Pat complied with the policies of that unit, to report all line of duty injuries, etc., no matter how minor. Well, in Rescue 2 we did not do that. Our "unwritten policy" was only to report injuries that required medical leave, but no one took the time to explain that to Pat. The officer whom Pat was working with was annoyed at the amount of paperwork Pat was producing—most of it minor injury stuff, but nevertheless, a report had to be filled out, etc. When the officer complained to me about it, I asked him if he had told Pat the policy of R-2. He said no.

Well, as fate would have it, Pat was working a mutual that night with me. Along about midnight, we had an ass-kicking job in a storage garage over in the Park Slope section of Brooklyn. We were in about fifty feet in pretty much zero visibility working with one of the local engine companies moving a line. Things began to deteriorate pretty fast, and the Chief ordered us out of the building. As we were crawling out, I hit my head on the lower portion of the garage door (the door was only up about two feet), knocking off my helmet, which rolled back into the garage. Pat, who was right next to me, did not hit the door and made it out a few seconds before me.

I got up and reported to the Chief without thinking of the helmet—I wanted him to know everyone was out (we were the last to exit—Rescue policy). Suddenly, I hear Pat who yells, "My lieutenant is still in there!" and immediately dives back into the garage. At this point, the fire was starting to come under the door. I dove after him, catching his leg and yelling to him, "Pat! I am out!" Pat backs out, holding my helmet. When we get away from the door, Pat is smiling. I am happy to get my helmet back and give him a big hug.

When we go back to quarters, Pat comes up to me and states he wants to put in a minor injury report for the job we just had. I asked him what was the injury, and he states he may have wrenched his back. I went to the office and proceeded to type out three reports—one, the fire report, two, the minor injury report for Pat, and three, a transfer request for Pat to leave the unit. I then called the troops to the office to discuss the fire, something we always did after a job.

As the men arrived in the office, I asked Pat to sign the reports. He signed the minor injury but froze when he saw the transfer request. He immediately asked, "Why?" I told him that while getting the personnel information to fill out the minor injury report, I noticed he had too many of them and figured working in such an active house was hazardous to his health, and if this continued, he would most certainly receive a more serious injury, and consequently, we would need a detail from a neighboring unit, and that could affect the cohesiveness of the unit, so maybe it would be better if he went back to Manhattan.

Pat looked at me with a shocked expression and immediately tore up the reports and apologized for not realizing what he was doing. As I left, I looked to my chauffeur and smiled—we got the message to Pat. And he was staying in the unit.

TOM KELLY – FDNY, Retired

I never worked directly with Patty; he was about fifteen years younger than me. One night, I'm working as a boss in 108 Truck, which at the time was a very busy house, very similar to Ladder 26. That night we catch a job; we walk to the fire floor and were getting ready to work our way into the apartment. And some guy comes out and *knocks* me down! Looks at me and says, "The place is all right."

And I, in my most pleasant way, tell him to get the fuck off the floor, what the hell are you doin' here, and the guy looks at me and goes, "You're Tommy Kelly." And I say, "Yeah, right." And he says, "It's Patty Brown!"

I says, "Yeah, Patty, get outta here!" I didn't know what the hell he was doin'. So anyway, we get in, the job is over, and I come downstairs and Patty is still waitin'. As I recall now, he was still in his shorts, it coulda been Bermudas or somethin' like that, but I go, "What the hell are you doin' here?" It was really (chuckle)—*not* a good block.

And he goes, "I *live* here—I live on the first floor."

JOE CURRY – Deputy Chief FDNY, Retired

I was one of Pat's first, if not *the* first, lieutenants he had as a member of Ladder 26 when he was a young firefighter. I assume he was still a probie. He was such a tenacious and terrific firefighter that our captain moved Paddy out of my group and put him in his own. I must admit I was annoyed at the time, but he was the captain, and it certainly was within his parameters to do what he did.

In one particular fire, Paddy must have had the OVM (outside vent man) position because after the fire was under control and we were in the process of overhauling, I heard that a member (unknown at the time) had fallen from a fire escape one story up. I never thought it was Paddy because I had just been talking to him via the H/T (handy-talkie), but sure enough, it was. When I bent down to him on the stretcher to see how he was doing, he apologized to me for falling off the fire escape. He had attempted to jump from one fire escape to the other and didn't quite make it. I said to myself right then that the biggest fear I had for Paddy was his being too aggressive, and getting seriously hurt or killed at some point in his career.

He was a model firefighter, and I feel privileged to have known him.

Medal Day **Magazine** – June, 1980

Fire was blowing out three windows on the fourth floor front, at 203 West 113th Street, as FDNY units rolled in. It was the early morning hours (2:12 a.m.) on March 7, 1980, and residents in night clothing were screaming for help. People were at windows and on the fire escapes of the six-story multiple dwelling as Ladder Company 26 went to work. A heavy smoke condition pushed through the top floors and the fire was extended to the fifth floor. Firefighter Patrick Brown of Ladder Company 26 was assigned "outside vent man" (vent the fire apartment from the exterior and conduct the necessary search and examination.) As Brown made his way up the front fire escape, he reached the fourth floor. At this

vantage point, he could hear cries for help, but could not see anyone. Passing the fire on the fourth floor, he moved up to the fifth.
More fire blew out the windows of the fourth floor, and the intense
heat forced him to the east end of the fire escape. From here,
Brown could now see three panic-stricken occupants directly above
him on the sixth (top) floor. Hose lines were not yet in operation
and conditions were worsening. Fire was now out the windows on
the fifth floor, preventing Firefighter Brown from using the stairs
up to the sixth-floor landing. Certain the victims were about to
jump, he acted in great haste to get up to them.

Quickly, he removed his mask and climbed up onto the fifth-
floor railing. From there, he jumped to the supports of the sixth
floor (fire) escape. By swaying back and forth, he got enough
momentum to swing himself over to the railing. He then pulled
himself up and over the railing and onto the fire-escape landing. He
now moved the victims out on the balcony, away from the main
body of fire. Shielding them from the unbearable heat, Brown
radioed for help. The aerial ladder climbed to assist Brown and the
three victims. Heavy smoke swirled about them, and due to the
dense smoke, it was necessary for Brown to direct the placement of
the ladder by using his radio.

The following remarks were made in the Deputy Chief's report
on this meritorious act: "Firefighter Brown exposed himself to
great danger due to the acrobatic nature that enabled him to reach
the victims. His composure enabled him to direct the chauffeur of
the Ladder Company in placing the aerial ladder under most trying
conditions. His actions were exemplary."

Pat Brown's rank at that time may have been second grade, but
his performance was first class. Working alone, Firefighter Patrick J.
Brown showed unique courage in attempting this rescue.

Journal Entry

Pat spent his entire life breaking the mold of a stereotypical firefighter. Perhaps the biggest dichotomy in his imaginary personals ad would be that when he wasn't swinging off fire escapes and crashing through windows to rescue people from flaming tenements, he was in a theatre seat, humming along to anything from "Old Man River" to "All That Jazz."

STEVE BAKER – Pat's Friend and AA Sponsee

Patty *loved* Broadway shows. He liked his musicals; his mother used to play piano. I think he wanted to come back to life as a choreographer. He thought the sexiest girls were the Bob Fosse dancers. He also respected how much work went into it. When he was around theatre people, that's when he'd act like a little boy—like, "I can't believe I'm here!"

Journal Entry – January 21, 2004

On a frigid, clear day I look out the train window onto the Hudson. Chunks of ice give solid testament to the weeks we've had of record cold. Hello, 2004. Brrrr.

I will be almost exclusively on the Upper West Side today. It is a neighborhood best encapsulated in memory as a ninety-degree day in 1978: I am armed with an iced coffee (one size only) from a neighborhood deli, and a double bill at the Thalia is the agenda for the afternoon. *Meet John Doe* or some other Frank Capra film, or maybe a screwball comedy with Jean Harlow or Carole Lombard. Somehow the depressed 1970s, the decade from which those early Hollywood classics provided escape, seem as long ago as the original Depression era itself.

Today generic high rises built for yuppies in the 80s line upper Broadway; their façades of Banana Republics and Ann Taylors and Starbucks gleam with the false glow of capped teeth. Braving baby-stroller gridlock, I will visit my friend Meredith, a wonderfully creative and vivacious cantor and mother of two little girls. We met in the early years of our karate training, and at one point (around one of those "big" birthdays) did the *New York Magazine* personals together. I was thirty-something, and my heart just wasn't in it. I judiciously snipped away at the self-description that would lure the perfect mate to answer my ad, more concerned with the cost per line than the prospects of Mr. Right seeing what a catch I was. Actually, I somehow knew that any meaningful relationship I might find myself in would be the result of kismet. And the personals just didn't fall under that heading.

Kismet. Soon after Pat and I met, at the first of what would be many dinners at Zinno's, his home away from home on that quiet and shady block of West 13th Street, we were comparing our likes and dislikes. Our first two dates did not include this sweet and normal prelude to a relationship. Pat had lost his friend, his "like a little brother" buddy Pete McLaughlin of Rescue 4, in a horrific fire just three days after our first date. Our initial bonding felt as if our very tears were mixing with his lifetime of loss and pain, forming an emotional epoxy that seemed tough enough to last forever. But on this particular evening, we had a normal follow-up date, where we shared our love of culture, specifically classic Broadway musical theatre. And when the giddiness of this discovery crested and I declared it "kismet," Pat informed me that he had that very CD, *Kismet*, on his player at home. And so, eager to prove it, he asked me to come back with him and see for myself. I laughed; it was such a cute variation on coming up to see his etchings. But when we got there, there it was. That antique of a show with songs that our mothers had played while we grew up in the 1950s, like "Bangles, Baubles and Beads," "Stranger In Paradise," and (the now ironically titled) "Don't Underestimate Baghdad." Well, don't underestimate the very real appeal of a handsome, macho-yet-sensitive firefighter who inherited a love of music from his gifted, beautiful, and ultimately troubled mother, who died far too young. What also got to me was the way he could shake up a tacky stereotype. The genie bottle I rubbed produced Pat Brown. Kismet it was.

Pat had friends who went back to the early 70s, difficult years he spent boxing, waiting to get admitted into the FDNY, and fighting the ghosts from Vietnam. Some were part of the Broadway theatre community, and Bill Cressler was one of them. Large in all senses of the word and full of an almost manic energy, Bill wanted to meet the person who was claiming so much of Pat's time and attention. We spent the evening with a pizza ordered in and the task of putting together a wooden file cabinet that Bill had given Pat for his birthday. It became evident that Bill was constantly giving or sending Pat gifts——"Quality Street" chocolates and shortbread from his many trips to London, bright red towels with "Captain" embroidered in the corner, and now this piece of furniture with dubious instructions and parts. Bill was very warm and welcoming toward me, something I can't say about all of Pat's older male friends. We hit it off, and how that file cabinet got assembled, I'll never know, because we ended up howling in laughter the entire time. What got the feat accomplished was maybe the sheer willpower of Pat combined with Bill's frenetic eagerness to see his gift ready to function as more tangible proof of his devotion to Pat.

I called Bill almost two years after 9/11, to see how he was faring and to let him know of my story-collecting project. Pat had several friends for whom I had special concern, given their attachment to him. Bill was top of the list. Pat once told me that he and Terry Hatton (a close friend of Pat and Captain of Rescue 1 at the time of 9/11) had to physically remove Bill from Pete McLaughlin's wake and slap him out of his hysterics. It took a while to get the nerve to check on Bill. When he returned my call, he seemed very intent on conveying how close he and Pat were, but in a manner and with details that suggested the need was greater to reinforce within himself than to inform me. By now I grasp the phenomenon. Not only am I encountering it in others, but I have experienced it personally. Who knew Pat best? Who loved Pat most? Who was closest, more deserving, more forgiving, more sensitive? Who understood Pat and was understood by Pat like nobody else? Perhaps the maddening and exquisite irony is that we *all* were. He had that quality of connecting one-on-one, with a deep current that tapped into something so universal, and yet so personal, that we all claim it even as we all share it.

I called Bill again last evening, to ask the location of the bench that was dedicated in Pat's honor by Bill and some theatre-world friends, near the Firefighter's Memorial on Riverside Drive. His sister answered. He had suffered a massive heart attack three days earlier, on a street in his neighborhood. His ashes are to be strewn into the Hudson. In June, when it is warm and ice-free and flowing down toward where the Towers once stood.

TOM O'KANE — Pat's Childhood Friend

I'm not surprised that Patty became the legend that he did, but I never saw him as a larger-than-life figure. I mean, I was his friend. I knew him all my life.

They'd have a Jamboree at the Fire Academy once a year—we were in the Explorers; that's how we met and got to be friends. I'd stay at his place in Queens, and he'd come to my house in the Bronx. My parents were divorced, and I spent a lot of time at my dad's firehouse.

Patty got onto the Fire Patrol. He was real young; I don't know how he got on it. They must have found out his age and told him to go get lost for a few years, or something. So he went into the Marines. That's my take on it.

He'd always donate his Medal Day award money to Odyssey House or some charity. I was always quietly amazed that he had that kind of character.

If somebody was in the water, drowning, I'd probably take my shoes off, empty my pockets first. He wouldn't. There would be no hesitation, and no consideration of the consequences. On the job, I don't know or think that he was ever out of position, but those same instincts probably made a difference in saving lives.

The gossip and innuendo and envy and jealousy that surrounded him then, and still do—I can't believe grown men are like that. I don't have to say, "Patty Brown's my best friend, blah, blah, blah..." Why all this nonsense?

Journal Entry – January 21, 2004, *continued*

I met John Rinciari at a diner in Chappaqua. What an unlikely setting for the two of us—John (or "Rince") with his Bronx working-class roots, and me with my general resistance to anything "Westchester County." But by happenstance, there we were, in our first get-together since the Explorers' Reunion that evolved from our first encounter, which was nothing less than an epiphany.

That was on a sweltering day in August. I got a call from a friend who owns a tasteful shop on Main Street, here in Beacon. It is filled with seeded glass urns, bamboo sushi trays, ornate picture frames, and ladies' hats. I had told Jacqueline about Pat prior to 9/11, as part of what two new acquaintances will do over a glass of wine—share some details of meaningful relationships as a type of initiation into the club of closer friendship. After the memorial services for Pat, I gave her his laminated mass card, which she posted above her desk in her shop. Our bonding continued in those two years, and I remember noticing the card still hanging that summer of 2003. I was touched, yet wanted to let her know it was okay if it was time for her to take it down.

JACQUELINE WEISSNER

I first learned about Pat Brown through you and your association with and love for Pat. And after 9/11, I shared your grief, and your loss suddenly became *my* loss. I don't know quite how to explain the whole thing, but there's something very special, some kind of magic that Pat Brown weaves amongst the living. It's almost like he's the Twenty-first Century Jesus, because he makes people feel things that you don't ordinarily feel for a total stranger. I've never met Pat, yet I feel I've known him for years. He has a strength and a kindness and an anger and a love that all of us really would benefit from having. Even the anger, because there's a pureness in Pat's anger that he's taken to a point that is no longer destructive; it's what drove him to be able to run into that building that horrible day and give his life.

One day you brought me his memoriam card. I've kept it on the wall in my shop because there's such a connection that I have for him—and some of it is explainable and some of it is not—this connection and protection and love and kindness that he emits even now. I said, "If it's okay, I really want to leave it up," and the picture has stayed on the wall.

So one weekend, this man and woman come through the door, we exchange hellos, and he starts walking around the shop and comes to the back where I'm sitting. He looks up, sees the card, and goes, "Who knew Pat Brown?" Scared the *hell* out of me!

"Uh…well…my friend Sharon knows Pat Brown, and I kind of know Pat through Sharon."

And with that, this strapping, robust man bursts into tears and tells me, "Pat Brown was the finest man walking the face of this Earth. He was my buddy in the Explorers. Every single day I miss him." And he's crying, and I'm now crying, and he then introduces himself as John Rinciari and extends his hand.

Since then I've had a couple of people come into the store who have seen his picture and say, "My husband worked with him!" or "I was supposed to go out with him; a girlfriend was going to set me up with him," or whatever. It's really kind of nice that there are a lot of people who know him, all of whom have nothing but kind words to say.

And I will never take that card down.

JOHN RINCIARI — Yonkers ESU Officer

I'm gonna go back to the beginning, when I first had the privilege of meeting Patty Brown. I was a twelve-year-old kid who aspired to be a New York City fireman, and as luck would have it, the FDNY sponsored an Explorer Scout program operating out of various firehouses. I was in the Bronx and belonged to Post 588, which was in Engine 88 on Belmont Avenue. Most of my friends, guys who are still my friends today, were part of that post. And we were real serious kids about being firemen—we ate, slept, and dreamt the FDNY. We looked up to the men in the firehouse in such a big way; they were a very big influence in our lives. We had such great and positive role models, something that's lacking with today's kids, and I consider myself very lucky to have had that.

The Fire Department Explorer program had competitions at The Rock, the Bureau of Training on Welfare Island (now Roosevelt Island), between Manhattan and Queens. So we'd go and compete. One group of kids from Queens and Brooklyn was a thorn in our sides, because we were really good and we knew it, but these other guys came in first. They were exactly the same kind of kids we were, in that they were really serious fire buffs.

And the main kid in that group was Patty Brown. I remember looking at him and always being kind of awestruck by his appearance—he was a miniature NYC stereotypical-looking fireman. He was the real deal. Patty was the main guy, the spokesman, the cog for the wheel. You couldn't help but like him, the kid was so enthusiastic. He emulated what we called the "heavy hitters," firefighters in the busy companies who were always making rescues, the real active gung-ho kind of guys. You could see how much Pat looked up to them. And we were kind of crazy buffs—we'd go anywhere to fires.

One of the guys' fathers had a contact at the training school at Welfare Island and made a deal with the fireman who was head of security there to allow us kids in with all our gear when The Rock was closed. We'd go there on holidays or weekends when there was nobody there, and this guy would let us in, and we'd have full run, unbeknownst to the FDNY. So many a day and night we spent out there, and no one knew. The whole thing was just make sure you put everything back where you got it before you left.

We did everything—roof rope evolutions, raised ladders, lit the smokehouse on fire, stretched lines into the smokehouse, and after a while, we really started to get a little pushy; we'd drive the apparatus around the island. For a long time, we got away with it. Patty's guys would meet us there, and we'd do this stuff together, fifteen to twenty kids. We were like "The Little Rascals" with access to all the stuff in the biggest fire department in the world.

One time us Bronx kids didn't show up, and that night, guys started getting phone calls from the firehouses: "What the hell did you guys do out at The Rock? Who messed up The Rock!" We didn't do anything—we weren't there, so it only could have been Patty Brown's guys. They found out his guys went out there that day, and it was a freezing cold winter day, and they had deck pipes going, and the old multiversal nozzles, and hand lines, and they flooded the training tower but some of the drains got clogged. The next day when the probie class came in, the entire thing was a sheet of ice. Years later, people would walk up to him and say, "Hey, Pat, did you turn The Rock into a skating rink lately?" But believe me, back then nobody thought it was funny. We thought it was going to be the end of our existence in the fire department. But Pat stood up and accepted the responsibility and the blame.

In October of 1966, twelve firemen were killed on 23rd and Broadway in a collapse, and we got excused from school to attend the funerals. I think ten out of twelve were at St. Patrick's Cathedral; I remember ten rigs with coffins on them. When we got down there, I remember standing next to Pat, talking to him, and seeing the aftermath horror of these guys killed in the line of duty, going by on the apparatus. After 9/11, I asked the FDNY pipe band if I could play the bagpipes with them for Pat's memorial service, and they said yes. I didn't think of it 'til I was standing in front of the church, that the last time I was there for a fireman's funeral was 1966, and I had stood next to Pat, and here I am now playing for him. It was very eerie, and very sad.

But a lot of things have happened after that, and it's almost like his spirit is buzzin' around somewhere and causing people to meet.

STEPHEN RACLAW — Suburban Milwaukee Firefighter/Paramedic
As a kid, instead of collecting baseball cards I collected stories of fires in the newspapers, and read *Firehouse Magazine* instead of *Sports Illustrated*. I

read about the Times Square roof rope rescue in 1991, and about the key players (Kevin Shea and Pat Barr), and of course, Pat Brown, who was the lieutenant in charge of Rescue 1 that day.

My senior year I was kind of going downhill, not paying attention to my studies. My sister's husband at the time knew a Yonkers ESU cop, John Rinciari, and we made a deal that if I pulled up my grades, he'd take me to New York for Easter break. John sent me a package of FDNY paraphernalia, along with *Medal Day* books where the name Pat Brown kept popping up. I realized that this guy was one dynamite firefighter. I also read an article about a big uproar over Pat being taken off the street and given a desk job. So I kind of followed his career without ever meeting the guy.

JOHN RINCIARI

Stephen was an avid Milwaukee-kid fire buff, and his dream was to come to NYC, hang out, and buff with the fire department. So I hooked him up with some of my friends and rode around with different firehouses. On his last day, I took him around the Bronx, Harlem, Manhattan, and the last stop was the Bronx fire headquarters where two of my good friends and fellow Explorers, Dennis O'Connell and Bobby "The Beef" Engel, were dispatchers.

So we go, "Okay, Stephen, you're going home tomorrow morning; is there anything that we missed?"

And he looks at me and says, "Hey, have you ever heard of this guy Paddy Brown?" So we started laughing, and Beefy gets on the phone and calls Pat at his firehouse.

After he talks to Stephen, Pat says to me, "Why the hell didn't you bring him down here? What the hell's wrong with you?"

STEPHEN RACLAW

I know I talked to him, but I don't know what I said. I mean, it was like talking to an idol. What do you say? I was seventeen at the time; I wasn't a fireman yet. I really wanted to meet him, but I never had the opportunity.

From that point on, I knew I wanted to be a great fireman. I knew I'd probably never be in New York or a big city, but you can be a great fireman in a small town. Not doing the things that he was, but you can make a difference. I read post-9/11 that he was great at encouraging his guys to do training, great as a mentor. Where I work, I'm one of the older guys at twenty-eight. There's a lot of younger guys, and I can try to be a mentor for them. For me, it's all about the Brotherhood, the welfare of the men—all the stuff Pat stood for. I never wanted to do anything else.

A year ago I was at the FDIC (Fire Department Instructor Conference) on the last day, making my last-rush purchases, and I noticed a booth that I hadn't seen before. They were selling bracelets for the victims of 9/11, and there were maybe two- to three-hundred bracelets, all lined up in five or six different rows. I just arbitrarily grabbed one and looked at it to see if it would stand up to what I would put it through. The woman running the booth asked who I was looking for, and I looked down and said, "This is the guy right here—Captain Patrick J. Brown, Ladder 3."

JOE LEETE – Division Chief of Training - Fairmount CO Fire Department
Not too long after we'd just met, Pat had to find out how serious I was about the FDNY. Every firehouse has a "home box," the number of the street alarm box closest to the station. After a couple of simple questions, Pat asked what my own home box was, and the corner it was on. Out of the blue. Those were answers that you had to know, basic ground level stuff, to even get started with Pat. I must have passed the test.

Pat was always on a bus or subway, to ride with a company somewhere in the city. Rescue 1, 26 Truck, and 31 Truck were his favorites. The busier the company, the more time Patty Brown spent there.

Firemen transferred from Manhattan and the Bronx to Engine 304 and Ladder 162 in Queens Village, get to know us, and Pat would immediately take advantage of every name he heard, go up and meet them just once, and be riding with them within minutes. We were at the firehouse one afternoon when an "all hands" rang in from Manhattan for a collapse. A second alarm came in just a minute later. Pat was off and running for the bus stop on Jamaica Ave.

"Rescue 1 will be there!" Forty-five minutes later we're standing at the corner, watching the rescue operation.

The phone rings at 8:15 on the most miserable, cold, rainy, windy Saturday morning that you can imagine, and it's Patty.

"Thirty-fifth Avenue and Utopia Parkway; the Engine called a second on arrival for a 'taxpayer.' We're taking the Q-27; meet us at Springfield and Hillside." Two buses and a long walk later, we are sitting on a multi-versal in front of a gutted grocery store.

Fifteen minutes later Pat says, "C'mon! There's a third on Intervale Avenue!" All wet and no fire wasn't Pat's style. The anticipation was the next best thing to the fight. We talked about the hazards, exposures, assignments, and tactics that might be used, during the trip to the job.

ALLEN (BUTCH) WILLIAMS – FDNY, Retired

Patty Brown was a *nut*! And so was I. So you'd put two nuts together, and you would have havoc. Some of the things that we did, you would not believe. We go back to the days before Pat was old enough to be an Explorer Scout. Patty used to hang around the Queens Village firehouse (Engine 302, Ladder 155) where I used to buff since I was a little kid. They started an Explorer Post there that was part of the citywide Fire Department Explorer Program. Harvey Moder was our leader.

In addition to the usual Scout things—mountain climbing, rappelling down the Palisades Mountains, overnight camping trips—we used to buff fires. Not only as individuals, but as a Scout group. When the twelve firefighters were killed on 23rd Street, in 1966, that night we buffed that fire. We eventually had our own truck—it was a Volkswagen open truck we built a cover on.

Patty and I would go to every big fire in the city. I had the fire radio; I would call up Patty, tell him we had a job in the Bronx, in Brooklyn. I would go from South Ozone Park, Queens, and pick up Patty in Queens

Village, and we would "respond." God knows how many times we'd turn around before we got there—they were already under control. And before that, when I wasn't even driving yet, we used to respond to fires, and we had our fire equipment in our duffle bags and traveled by train. We could never understand why the fires were out and most of the guys had taken up by the time we got there. But we tried. And we actually made a few fires.

One job we made—we traveled to Harlem during the 1968 riots. We went from tenement to tenement, from fire to fire, searching to make sure nobody was in. And this was long before the apparatus ever got there—no fire trucks around. People out on the street were rioting, the place was going crazy, and the only thing that stopped us was four flat tires, from all the glass in the street. I ended up abandoning my father's car, and we had to take the train home. But we stuck it out, we stuck it out 'til the car literally couldn't move anymore. And that's why I say Patty's a nut, because traveling over to Harlem in the middle of a riot, running around to fires like that—you can't be totally sane.

There was another job right by the firehouse where we had the Explorer program, and I had just gotten in the Fire Department; Patty wasn't in yet. We were driving along, and I said, "Patty, there's smoke coming out of that house!" So we pulled a box, and then we went in and made a search. Being very intelligent firefighters, we knew the house was heavily charged, and we didn't want it to light up, so we went in the house and closed the door behind us. And made a search with no ventilation. Choking, gagging on the floor, but neither one of us was gonna back down because the other one wasn't gonna back down. So we became very tough firefighters, and I think that was the beginning of showing our toughness at fires. And Patty kept going 'til 9/11.

FRANK BENDL – Pat's Childhood Friend
Patty knew what he wanted to be at a very, very early age, and the reason I say that is because when you're in the fifth grade, and you have a fire

department scanner, which you got for your birthday, and the firehouse is two blocks from your house, and you got the fire trucks goin' all over, and you're racin' on your banana bike followin' the firemen to fires; and when you come to school late, smellin' like the fire, with a note from your mother—I think you know that you're gonna be a fireman. There was no question what Patty was gonna be. He longed to be a fireman, and he became *the* fireman of firemen. The legend. That was Patty Brown.

JOHN RINCIARI

When Pat was a probie, there was a guy, Eddie Beban, in my neighborhood on Decatur Avenue in the Bronx who was a fireman in 26 Truck in Harlem, and I heard that Pat was going there after probie school.

So I see this guy and go, "Hey! My buddy's gonna be in 26; he's a probie. His name's Patty Brown."

And he said, "Oh, yeah, okay," and kinda didn't pay much attention to it.

A while goes by and I'm comin' down the street, and I hear this guy callin' to me: "Hey! Rince!" And comes up to me. "*You* better have a talk with your friend, that guy Patty Brown! He's fuckin' crazy!"

I go, "Whaddya mean?"

"He's climbing up the sides of buildings, swinging off fire escapes— he's gonna get himself killed!"

And I just looked at him and said, "Hey, you better get used to it— that's Patty Brown!"

Pat was the kinda guy that if I hadn't seen him in a long time and happened to run into him, it was like we never missed a beat. He turned out to be a combination of all those "heavy hitters" that he looked up to; Patty worshiped those guys, and that's what he turned out to be in his own life. I was always just really proud of him.

JOE LEETE

In 1974, New York City nearly went bankrupt; cops and firemen were being laid off, and I went to work for EMS for a little over four years.

Unfortunately, my eyesight kept me from any civil service job in New York City. After taking a burn victim to the NYU Burn Center one night, I picked up a *Rocky Mountain News* lying there, and saw dozens of fire department jobs advertised. Contact lenses were allowable, and I'm still out here, almost thirty years later.

There's a lieutenant on the department here who went back to Manhattan several years ago to a safety symposium and coincidentally heard Patty speak. He returned to Colorado wanting to change things overnight, and told me, "So *that's* the guy. Now I see what drives you. Now I know where it comes from."

Firefighters have a sense about officers like Pat Brown. Other fire officers who knew Captain Patrick Brown know that they cannot emulate him just from hearing or reading of him. Having literally grown up in the fire service, Pat learned many lessons the hard way. As a teenager, Pat heard things in firehouse kitchens that he knew he should not have. He never repeated them. As a company officer, he witnessed wrongs and tried to right them, but he never badmouthed the Department.

Newly promoted men and women look up to their officers for motivation and guidance. Pat's lessons continue to teach us to provide that, and more: be consistent, fair, and compassionate officers, while we just be ourselves at the same time.

"...the growth of understanding follows an ascending spiral rather than a straight line." —JOANNA FIELD

Journal Entry – January 30, 2004

Another crystalline winter day—my 9:05 commuter train makes its way along the Hudson from Beacon toward the city, and I, sitting on a backward-facing seat, look to my left and squint against the brilliance of ice on the river. The trees are delicately etched against the white rocky landscape looming to the west. Bannerman's Castle appears, stark and strange as if it drifted from some medieval dream and froze in place with the river current. West Point, opposite Garrison, is a catapult's throw downstream, and following that is Indian Point, the nuclear plant that seems perpetually to have a big red arrow over it beckoning Osama bin Laden to wreak yet more havoc.

I was going to drive in today but didn't trust my luck on the Parkway with the recent snow and the old ice, summing up what has been a solid month of sub-freezing temperatures. I'm not experienced enough with winter driving, I defy the gods by not owning a cell phone, and besides, I want to go to a bar in the city—The Bravest—for Happy Hour, and hang out a bit where Pat used to be a bouncer circa 1980. Then it was called Suspenders.

WANDA SHADWICK – Pat's Friend from Suspenders

Pat was one of a few of us who worked Sunday evenings. It was our favorite night; we'd all have our dinner together first, while it was quiet and slow. Up 'til a point. Then "they" would come. There was an est meeting group around the corner on 38th Street, and they would eventually break for dinner. We dreaded it, *every* Sunday. Patty would be there at the door, in his black turtleneck and jeans, with his serious face: "You ready? They're comin'!"

Zoom! Zoom! Every table was full. They didn't go to the bar, because they weren't drinking. Part of their training is that they cannot go to the bathroom. And they were trained to be assertive and to speak up and say exactly what they wanted; that's how I understood it. And they were only allowed so many minutes before they had to get back. I don't remember if it was thirty minutes, or forty-five, but it was very hard for us to serve everybody, all together. And every week, as we got used to the est group, we'd start grumbling, "The hell with them! We're only human; we're not gonna put up with this!" But the bosses loved it, 'cause they packed the place.

So there were two girls waitressing; I worked this side of the dining room. One little table had a man who came in by himself. He sat there and put his fist down, and ordered a cheeseburger.

I said, "Okay, how would you like that cooked?"

He goes, "No, I've changed my mind. I don't want a cheeseburger." And the assertiveness was coming out, and his voice started getting louder.

"Okay, what would you like, sir?"

"I'll have a steak."

And I said, "That comes with a salad and French fries."

Then he says, "I don't want the salad. No, I don't want the French fries. I'd like a baked potato."

So I tell him, "That can be done, but you only have so many minutes, correct? So, it's gonna take some time."

"Well, I want what I want, and I want it *now!*"

His voice is getting louder, and I'm getting a little upset and angry, and

I say, "Sir, if you only have thirty minutes, you're better off getting the cheeseburger——"

"I just *told* you what I want, and I want you to get it *now!*"

"Um, sir, you're not going to get your baked potato in time."

"What did I just *tell* you?" and his hand started coming toward me.

It was so fast, but I saw the blur of another hand grab his hand, and Patty is standing there saying, "You aren't gonna do what I think you're gonna do?" And as he was doing that, his other arm was pushing me out of the way.

I believe the guy urinated in his pants. All of that est training, all those hours he paid for... Just went right out the window.

Patty, seething, goes, "You know what? You won't be eating here tonight. You'd better leave right now."

I said to Patty, "Thank you! But...where did you come from?" He was like a ninja!

He goes, "I watch *every*thing. I know everything that's going on."

Just before Pat gave up drinking, I remember him saying, "I'll be here all night, and I'll just end up sleepin' all day. I'm just wastin' time. There's better stuff out there."

That was when he got more involved with things like Broadway shows; there was a whole new world out there for him, and he seemed to be very happy. He joined AA and made a million-zillion friends with that. And, of course, he stayed away from Suspenders for a while, because this was a trigger. The only time I saw him was when he was running or bicycling by. He'd stop, and I'd come out to the sidewalk saying, "No hugging until you get rid of the sweat!" And he'd laugh.

I always let him know about our parties and anniversaries; I would invite him for a couple of years, to give him the choice. I wanted to let him know we were always thinking about him. But he never showed up.

At the end, I think he missed a lot of the people. Not the drinking, but the people themselves. Not long before 9/11 I saw him outside. He seemed so melancholy.

He said, "Wanda, if you have anything goin' on here—any party or anniversary—make sure you call me, 'cause I really feel like seein' everybody." The next one would have been Christmas, 2001.

I always feel that people get premonitions before they die, and I wonder...

Journal Entry – February 8, 2004

I open the Sunday *New York Times* and am bombarded with them: Valentine's Day ads—assaults and insults to those of us with broken hearts. But there was a time, eight years ago to be exact, when I was someone's Valentine.

Pat worked most holidays to give other guys in the firehouse the chance to be with their families. Valentine's Day 1996 was no exception. So we met on the 15th, for dinner at a place he had picked, the Miracle Grill. He told me he had first seen me there, dining on the patio with friends on a spring day, several years before. It was a Mexican restaurant, low-key in that East Village style, and over enchiladas he asked me to marry him.

The symbol of this gesture was his USMC dog tag. I remember touching the embossed initials and numbers tentatively, the tag itself almost weightless, paradoxically, compared to the promise and hope of our future together. He said it was just a stand-in until we got a ring. The next day we shopped and found a silver bead chain on Christopher Street. I looped the tag through and wore it with more pride than any Tiffany diamond or Mikimoto pearl.

I still have it. I touch the letters, tenderly now, and occasionally wear it on personal special occasions.

Today, however, Kirk has sent me a gift—two boxes of Daffin's "Meltaways" made locally in Youngstown, Ohio, where he plays harp and teaches yoga. Kirk himself is a gift from Pat. For comfort after 9/11, I would turn to the Internet tribute sites and read things at times so personal that they seemed meant to be beamed straight to the heavens. But there they were, in cyberspace, for anyone to be audience to.

And there Kirk Kupensky shared eloquently of first reading about Pat in a *Yoga Journal* article that ran in December 2001.

A week before 9/11, I ran into Pat on the street, his yoga mat rolled up under his arm and his step quickening, ready to jog the eight blocks from Ladder 3 to Jivamukti Yoga Center. "I'm going to be in *Yoga Journal*," he said, beaming with an almost childlike pride, and he whipped out a photo proof taken in his firehouse with his FDNY tank top and his yoga mat. When Pat was happy, tapping into that energy would always recharge your good-mood batteries. And so I retained a smidge of that positive flow when soon after 9/11, I e-mailed the magazine to let them know just how happy and proud Pat had been the last time I saw him. When the issue ran, the editor noted that her decision to run the story after learning his fate was based on an e-mail (mine, I presumed, though I have heard from others who make the same claim. We can all share the credit). So Pat's energy went through the channels and reached other people…including Kirk.

KIRK KUPENSKY

Add me to the list of people who wish they had known Paddy Brown. Like many others, his death—and his life—haunt me. I first heard about him in an article in *Yoga Journal* magazine. Accompanying the article was a beautiful photo of him wearing leggings and an FDNY tank top with his hands in prayer position. Before I even read the article, I was struck by the look in his face and eyes—I could tell that this man had a story to tell. What had those eyes seen or that body endured that could only be imagined by me?

Upon reading the article, I learned he was a former Marine, Vietnam vet, and most- decorated NY fire captain. Pretty hairy-chested stuff to be sure—but then I read about the man who cried the first time he chanted in a yoga class, who went on to describe how yoga helped him emotionally and spiritually. It occurred to me that this man had found the balance that all men strive for or struggle with—that of acknowledging their aggressive sides with their emotional, spiritual sides, then blending the two into a unified whole in service to others.

This is my definition of a "real" man.

In this magazine article, I certainly had found someone whom I could relate to, but yet I felt that something was horribly, terribly wrong. The article made no mention of Patrick's fate, and it wasn't until reading the editor's comments at the front of the magazine that I did learn of him rushing into the World Trade Center, trying to reach those who couldn't help themselves, and then perishing when the building collapsed.

Neither I, nor my own yoga practice, have been the same since. For it is in yoga that I become aware of my own physical strength and my "be-ingness" as an entity on this planet. The two must not be separated, but integrated to reach a state of wholeness. From there, you take what you learn, apply it to your life, reaching out to others. This is the yoga (or "union") that I strive for, having found the most stunning manifestation of it in the life and death of Captain Patrick Brown.

I mourn the fact that I will never know him on the physical plane. I like to think that we would have gotten along well, with lots of ideas to share.

Recently, I've been approached with a request to teach yoga to a group of men as well as to a group of firefighters. Coincidence? I'd like to think not. I will always carry the memory of Paddy Brown with me on the yoga mat, and will share his story with my students. Being human, I'm sure that Pat had his fair share of mistakes, foibles, maybe even regrets. I won't take these away from him—but I do believe that he did reach a state of perfection in his life and death. I pray that he will continue to teach me, and the rest of us here.

FELISE (SHIVADASI) BERMAN —Yoga Instructor

I was not prepared for the everlasting imprint of Patrick's life on my heart. Patrick and I frequently spoke before yoga class and shared our own personal life stories. When I invited him to attend my teachers' graduation at Jivamukti, he said he was sure to be there, and added, "I need the right date, Felise, so I can get the guys at the firehouse to cover me that night." He sat in the front of the room with so much sincerity; it was so sweet to have him there.

I once said to Patrick, "You should become a yoga teacher."

He shyly replied, "I can't even touch my toes."

But he was far more of a yogi than he knew.

JOSH GOSFIELD – Fellow Yoga Practitioner (excerpt from video tribute to Pat)

Halfway through my first yoga class, my clothes were soaked, my lungs were heaving, and my head was about to explode. Wiping the sweat from my eyes, I marveled at the twenty-two-year-old girls all around me, effortlessly contorting themselves into impossible positions. Although you'll hear a lot of talk at the yoga studio about inner peace and loving your fellow man, it's not the kind of place where strangers say hello. So I was surprised when you came up to me one day and said, "Hi. I'm Pat." I knew you. You were the guy in the back with the crinkly smile, who was as stiff as me.

The day I saw the insignia on your shirt, I thought, what the hell is a fireman doing in a yoga class? But when I asked if you were, you said, "Yeah. I am." I didn't know then that you were famous among the other firemen for your daring raids into burning buildings to save lives.

I always said, "Hi, Pat," and "Bye, Pat" to you before and after classes. But I won't be seeing you around any more.

Now I keep running into people who knew you. I keep hearing stories about Patty Brown. But you won't be going to sing any Irish music or teaching karate to blind kids, or rushing into burning buildings. And you're never there in the yoga class anymore. Your usual place in the back is taken by someone else.

I never could have stood in your shoes. But when I move into a downward dog, a warrior, a crow, or a wheel, I think about you, Pat, wherever you are. Bye, Pat.

PAT BROWN – *NBC, Today Show* – Summer, 2001 (Interview from a segment filmed at Jivamuki Yoga Center)

What is your name and occupation?

My name is Patrick Brown and I'm a Captain in the New York Fire Department.

What got you into a yoga class?

Personally, I was kinda worried, afraid to start this stuff, 'cause I thought, I'm not flexible, I'm all banged up. I'd run for twenty years; I did twenty-five years of boxing and karate-stuff, and twenty-five years with the fire department, and a tour in Vietnam. My body was pretty shot. I initially came here because of the physical aspect, because I learned that yoga would help rejuvenate your joints and your bones and stuff like that. And that's pretty much what it's done, but it's done a lot more for me in a lot of different ways that I really didn't expect.

What are the unexpected benefits of yoga you personally experienced?

The first day I came here, about a year and a half ago, Kristin was teaching, and she got out that little piano-thing (harmonium), and she started singing. And I started crying! I didn't expect that, in a yoga class; I knew that this was a physically tough discipline. And then she gave this nice little beautiful speech about the philosophy and stuff, ya know, and it kinda really helped me out in a lot of ways. It was funny, 'cause I started cryin' and then ten minutes later I was sweatin' my brains out, just struggling to stay afloat in there.

It's kinda crazy—when I first got there, it was really difficult just to get through a class. Now that I'm here a year and a half, I'm gettin' a little bit of a sense of how to do it, it's even more difficult, but in a more focused kind of way.

SHARON GANNON – Co-founder, Jivamukti Yoga Center

Pat came here just about every day. And he always came at least a half hour before the class he was going to take. He'd sit quietly on one of the benches—I don't know if I could say that he was meditating. He might have been. But he certainly was not an asocial person, because if anybody came up to talk to him, he would then become completely engaged, and very animated, and very giving, in conversation. But, for the most part, he came and sat there by himself. That's how he prepared to take the class. And he always put his mat in the same place, in the back of the room.

Once a film crew was filming a class I happened to be teaching. The producer asked if anybody wanted to stay after, for more intensive interviews. So they chose five people, and Pat was one of them. Three of those chosen were Jivamukti teachers. Now, every month we have a theme that we teach from, and that month it was vegetarianism. So that was the talk that I had given at the beginning of class. And always, whenever I am given a microphone, or a chance to get some kind of press, I try to mention the animals and a vegetarian lifestyle. Naturally, I thought, this would be a great opportunity.

The producer asked something like, "What benefits have you discovered through your practice of yoga?" I'm standing there, hoping that every one of these five people is going to talk about vegetarianism. Since three of them are teachers, I figure of course they'll talk about it! But—no! The first person talked about healing an injury, the second, about losing weight and gaining confidence, and on and on—the kinds of things that, generally, you associate perhaps with yoga. I was very disappointed that even the teachers were just offering pretty superficial answers.

Well, last up was Pat Brown. Now I knew, because we had talked about it before, that Pat was not a vegetarian. So I thought, well, I'm not going to hear what I want from Pat Brown. Okay, fine. Pat started speaking, about the fact that yoga had transformed his life on every single level.

"I'm not a complete vegetarian, now. But, because of the relentless teachings that we receive here, and the fact that I have faith in what I am being taught—I am experimenting with it. And I am proud to say that I am working very hard toward that, and it is a goal for me. And I believe it is the way to go."

He went on to say that "yoga takes courage, because you really are confronted with your own perceptions of who you think you are, what you're capable of. And it takes a lot of courage to meet those kind of challenges, much more than going into a burning building, sometimes."

He had this total faith in the method of yoga, and I had the impression that that was how he approached everything. That once he committed to something, he was going to go one hundred percent. He didn't then stop, and say, "Well, I don't know…" When you said, "Handstand," he would just do it. He might not be really picture-perfect, but he didn't sit there and go, "You gotta be kiddin.'" That was his signal for, I'm gonna try. I'm gonna put my whole heart and my whole soul into this, and I'm gonna do my best. And that's what he did with every single part of the yoga class.

DAVID LIFE – Co-founder, Jivamukti Yoga Center

I practiced next to him a lot, almost more than teaching him. Often, I would help him, if he was having difficulty in a pose—I'd just jump in and hold his leg, or whatever was needed.

Your progress depends on your clear intention, how often you practice, and how much fervor you have. Pat excelled in all those areas, so he made progress very fast.

I never talked to him about his personal life, or anything much at all, but I could see the change, the revolution he underwent. When he first started coming, there was a kind of dark quality, a suffering quality, a rigidity. But soon his face relaxed, his body became much more smooth and at ease, and he seemed to drop his emotional/psychological armor. That's not something I talked to him about, but rather something I observed in him.

We deal with archetypes in yoga that represent the postures, not just physically but energetically and emotionally; they are helpful to a person's development. One of these is the Hero. "Virasana" means Hero Pose (in Sanskrit). It means that you sacrifice your personal comfort and welfare so that others can be free. We talked about it a lot in class, and I can just see him now, sitting there, smiling.

He took his role so seriously and so fully. It wasn't just a pastime, waiting for life to happen. It was "real time."

BEAZER PITIGER – Fellow Yoga Practitioner

At a four o'clock Jivamukti yoga class one afternoon, I noticed a fellow about my age. (I am fifty-six; most of the others are younger.) And oddly enough, although we didn't say anything, we sort of acknowledged each other. One day we started to talk, and we discovered that we were both Marine Corps veterans of the same outfit in Vietnam. Pat was junior to me, so he was in-country toward the end, around the early 70s.

Then I told him I was one of the lobbyists for disabled veterans in the state of New York, and he told me about his career, that he was a captain in the fire department. And he gave me a little background of how he came through the ranks, and that he was with Special Operations Command (S.O.C.) a lot of times.

I said, "There's a fellow that lives across from my sister in Deer Park, Long Island, who's also with S.O.C. in the fire department." And his name was Ray Downey. Ray Downey was Pat's mentor in Rescue 2, and had trained him. So another connection was established.

On September 11, I was out running on the west bank of the Hudson, in Jersey City. I saw the plane hit the North Tower. Then I saw the other plane hit the South Tower. And for some reason I knew in the epicenter of my being that Pat Brown was down there. When the North Tower collapsed, I had this chill—there's a sound that the Sikhs use; the sound is a call that means "deathless"—run through my body. I knew that Pat Brown was there and wasn't going to make it through.

I later found that Pat had given his life for the greater good once again, and I was deeply affected. It was a privilege to have met this guy, and in the same short time that we knew each other, to share the same space doing yoga, and talk about spiritual endeavors with him, and just get a sense of who he was and how far he had come from growing up in a

Roman Catholic background, trying to transcend some of the cultural ties that bind us to prejudicial outlooks in life.

I knew that it was Pat Brown's funeral mass that was gonna stop the streets. I attended the mass, along with thousands of firefighters, not only from New York but all over the US and Canada. It was an especially moving time for me, because at that point I think I transcended a lot of death experiences that I was hanging on to from Vietnam. I was able to let go of a lot of old, festering wounds.

I was sitting in the back of the cathedral, trying to be as inconspicuous and anonymous as possible. It was the most heartrending eulogy that I had ever experienced. You got a real sense of who this man was, the caliber of this man, how he lived his life. Furthermore, you realized the loss, not only to his family, but to the whole community.

This being a Roman Catholic service, we were up and down a lot; I mean, we were standin' up, sittin' down, standin' up, sittin' down— the whole dogma thing. And at the very end, when people were filing out, we stood for the last time, and then sat down once again. My mind was going up to the ceiling; I was trying to get beyond the earthly appearance of this place and to what was really behind the religion, looking up at the stained glass.

Then we stood up, and I heard this metallic ping. I was really perplexed—I wasn't quite sure what it was. The firefighters next to me filed out, and I was the only one in the pew. I'm looking around, and I see underneath my feet are these captain's bars. And I picked them up and just held onto them.

ELLEN WOOD – Author's Friend – Friday, November 9, 2001
New York City said goodbye today to Captain Patrick J. Brown of Ladder 3. To his fellow firemen, he was "Paddy." To the rest of us who were privileged to have known him, he was just Pat.

Today would have been his forty-ninth birthday. It was one of those days that make "autumn in New York" famous—impossibly clear blue skies, the air both crisp and clean. Very much as it was the morning of September 11th, the day that Pat Brown died.

We gathered on the steps of St. Patrick's to await his funeral cortege. Two fire trucks parked across the street from the cathedral steps, in front of the bronze statue of Atlas that guards the entrance to Rockefeller Center. They raised their tall ladders, crossed them gently, as soldiers arched their swords, and hung an American flag at their crest. I don't know why the image of Atlas bearing the world upon his shoulders reminded me of Pat, but it did. And everywhere, as far as the eye could see, both up and down 5th Avenue, there were lines of firefighters in dress uniform, perhaps six to eight deep. It didn't seem possible that we had so many firefighters in New York, and I later found out that some of them had come from as far away as California and Nevada to bid Pat farewell. There were tourists, too, who waited politely behind the police barricades to pay their respects. An ocean of comrades, a sea of friends and strangers stood together in his honor. And then something utterly extraordinary happened. New York City gave Pat the rarest gift of all: silence. This was midtown at midday on a weekday, and there was not a sound to be heard anywhere.

There wasn't a coffin, of course. Two horses preceded the bagpipers, who played a lament as a truck from Ladder 3 quietly followed. Pat's men, or rather, those who did not die with him, walked behind the truck. I've forgotten how many of Ladder 3's firefighters died that day—I believe it was twelve. The numbers begin to blur, after a while.

The church itself, seemingly so large, was filled to capacity. Many had to listen to the service from outside, where it was broadcast by speakers on the cathedral steps. It was a grand mass, as grand as they get. Several priests consecrated the Eucharist; Cardinal Egan sat to the side and watched over the proceedings. The American Boys' Choir performed; a fireman with a beautiful tenor sang "Ave Maria." But these are all things that belong to the services of the church; the eulogies belonged to Pat.

Mayor Giuliani, former Governor Carey, and Fire Commissioner Von Essen praised him as the brave, courageous warrior that he was—not only in his life as a fireman, but as a soldier before that in Vietnam, during an era when serving one's country was not a respected career option. He was a hero, of course. He was a man who lived his life on the front line always, and was at home there. But talk of heroism was something he left for others. The Pat I knew would chat amiably over dinner about how he'd seared his ear the night before at work, yet the only thing that marked the event as extraordinary in his mind was that he'd gotten scorched, not that he'd gone charging into an inferno. That part of the job was a given.

And that point was made clear by the others who eulogized him, including his brother Mike, his friend Mike Daly of the *NY Daily News*, and Mike Moran of Ladder 3. They brought to life the human side of Pat Brown, and we all laughed at Daly's tales of Pat's idiosyncrasies, which were so much a part of his charm. Moran, famous for declaring that "Osama Bin Laden can kiss my royal Irish ass" at the Concert for New York City, wept as he told us that it was fitting that Pat was the last of the Ladder 3 men to be buried, as Pat was always the last man out at a fire. We all wept with him. Pat's men would have followed him into the mouth of Hell, and at the very last, they did.

He was a fireman's fireman. At the reception following the funeral, an entire ballroom filled with his fellow firefighters surged to its feet and cheered as some of his most daring exploits were replayed in a video tribute to his life. But in the end, Pat belonged to all of New York, and was as revered by its people as he was by his men. After the funeral, I watched as an old man in the crowd saluted him, tears streaming down his face. He wasn't the only ordinary citizen to do so.

I'm not a religious woman. The church and I parted ways many years ago. Yet one particular prayer, uttered by the priest who conducted Pat's funeral, keeps ringing over and over again in my heart:

"Let us pray that we, the people of the City of New York, and that we, as citizens of this great nation, make ourselves worthy of all of those who died for us that day."

I can add only this: "Amen."

"If you want to win anything—a race, your self, your life—you have to go a little berserk." —William Shakespeare

Journal Entry – February 11, 2004

Seeing the Broadway revival of the 1950's musical *Wonderful Town* today was a sort of Valentine gift to myself. I went with Nancy, an old roommate from my art-student days, so this show about two sisters trying to "make it" in the Big Apple (before that advertising slogan was even a seed) seemed nostalgic and timeless all at once.

Those shudders that can unexpectedly reverberate to your core—what exactly are they? With me, they happen so often with music. A note is sung, it strikes an emotional keyboard, and tears well up for no rational reason.

Pat would have loved this show. I felt him there with me in the center front mezzanine so strongly that I could hear him humming along. He would have informed me that the lead, Donna Murphy, had also won a Tony award for Stephen Sondheim's *Passion*, not because he read it in the *Playbill* but because he had seen her in the show, and had bought the CD to play at home. He used to go to the theatre by himself, many times right after a tour, still in his FDNY uniform. And Stephen Sondheim was his favorite composer/lyricist. No fluffy escapism fills his art of adult-relationship portrayal; a witty darkness and sad cynicism permeate his words with a grim reality that Pat could identify with. There was no "happily-ever-after-ing" with Sondheim. And that gave a kind of validity and resonance to Pat's personal experiences with disappointments in love.

We had seen a revival of *Company* in London, which was my first real introduction to Sondheim. Later, after I memorized the score, and with great exuberance in sharing my enthusiasm with Pat, I asked him what song was his favorite. With no hesitation, he said "Being Alive."

STEPHEN SONDHEIM – "Being Alive"

Somebody hold me too close
Somebody hurt me too deep
Somebody sit in my chair
And ruin my sleep
And make me aware
Of being alive

Somebody need me too much
Somebody know me too well
Somebody pull me up short
And put me through Hell
And give me support
For being alive

Make me confused
Mock me with praise
Let me be used
Vary my days

But alone is alone, not alive...

Somebody crowd me with love
Somebody force me to care
Somebody make me come through
I'll always be there
Frightened as you
To help you survive
Being alive.

Journal Entry – February 21, 2004

Winter still has its death grip on me, turning my moods into dingy grey ice banks that refuse to melt in my emotional landscape. The promise of daffodils is not even a mirage on my mind's horizon.

There is a documentary about Pat in the works. Steve McCarthy is making it, and he asked if I would contribute with a filmed interview. The working title is *Finding Paddy*. Initially, it was to be about Mike Brown, after driving cross country to dig for Pat at Ground Zero, looking for his older brother who in many ways he never really knew, and subsequently finding out from people bits and pieces of who Pat was. Or so I assume. But Mike has aborted, and who can blame him? The post-9/11 stress he's been under for so long, on top of that which he regularly encounters in his job as an ER doctor in Las Vegas, has caused a shift to its now being Steve's quest.

Steve had done several *Dateline NBC* shows featuring Pat; the first was after the Watts Street fire in 1994, where Pat took care of Captain John Drennan's family and sat vigil with his horrifically burnt friend for forty days and nights until Drennan's death. The second *Dateline* was started before and finished after 9/11. In the course of filming, Steve, too, was drawn in by Pat. I trust Steve, and sense that he will try and get to the essence of Pat, whose early trauma and personal struggles provided the very fodder for attaining his professional heights and searching his soul as deeply as the journey went, for inner peace. Steve is open to me and my experience. It is a breath of fresh air.

I last saw Steve at a reunion at an American Legion Hall on City Island in November, 2003. I was surprised that he was there, with his camera in tow. It was to be an intimate gathering of people who had known and worked with Pat, going back as far as the Boy Scouts Explorer program. But due to the fact that it was honoring Pat, some "usual suspects" inevitably turned up. Mostly not from the FDNY, but people who met Pat after he joined AA and became sober and was well on his way to becoming a legend in the department.

They probably knew each other slightly when Pat was alive, but I doubt much occasion arose for them all to be in the same room. Actors, journalists, filmmakers, firefighters. They grew tighter after Pat's death, drawing in as a wound knits while healing. The memorials, anniversaries, and tributes kept happening; the need to join and be communal persisted, with sadness being the common water we all still tread.

I say "we" but it is them, and me. It is very much a boys' club. They are polite to me, and there is a little chit chat, an air-kiss, but not once has any of them really engaged with me or even asked me a personal question. Not about Pat and me. Not regarding my trip to Vietnam last year, based on Pat's stay in-country. And nothing about my current project of collecting stories. I sense that they really don't know what to make of me. Maybe they have made a collective judgment about the women in Pat's life, that we are loose cannons, not to be trusted with the memory of Pat. Maybe they transfer over their own relationship issues. For a while, I gave them the benefit of the doubt and thought perhaps I imagined it all. I am pretty benign and low profile, as Pat's women go. Then again, I am the woman he asked to marry. But still, that protective/possessive drawbridge is pulled up, and I am on the opposite side of the moat. That fortress to Pat's memory, with its guardsmen who lionize Pat's gift of empathy to the point of martyrdom, keeps me at bay while they are on watch. I would need nothing short of a Trojan horse to be allowed to enter, but that doesn't interest me. I have my own memories, and liken them to a public garden, open to visitors for certain hours, but closing at dusk...

STEVE McCARTHY

I'm a television producer, in the TV business since 1981, and in 1990, I was working for FOX Television for that show, *America's Most Wanted*. The executive producer wanted to branch out, so I said, why not do a *COPS*-style show about firefighters? So we started kicking around ideas, and one day he said, "There was this amazing rope rescue in Times Square, and it's on tape! Build your own story so that it ends with this incredible thing, because you could wait for months and never get such a rescue captured on videotape."

I called the department, who sent me up to Rescue 1, and it turned out one of the guys who was the lieutenant in charge of the roof rope rescue was Paddy Brown, a lieutenant in Rescue (S.O.C.) So we began to film, which meant, sort of, me bedding with Rescue 1. I got to know all the guys, but there was something about Paddy that I sensed immediately—this sort of deep character, in many ways—I didn't know what, but first of all, he was very handsome. Second of all, he was in command, and he was very telegenic; the camera loved him. And as we got to talking, it turned out that his father was an FBI agent, he grew up in Queens. My father was a cop, and I grew up in Brooklyn. We had a lot of similarities, both borough guys.

We did finish the piece, and he was one of the stars, of course, and we stayed in touch after that, maybe three times a year. I really didn't know too much about him. He would tell me a little bit about Vietnam, about growing up. Certainly about the job. But we did talk about doing a movie, and he said a really good friend of his, an actor, wanted to write a screenplay, and I said some day we'd do it.

So in 1994, I see in *The New York Times* a picture of him and Vina Drennan, and I call him up and say, "What's happening?" And, "Do you think she'd want to do a story?" I went to Captain John Drennan's wake and I met Vina for the first time. And then we started to shoot the story that became the *Dateline NBC* story about her vigil for her husband, and her relationship with Paddy. We edit the piece together, and it wins an Emmy, and people are like, "Who is this guy, Paddy Brown?"

So we stay in touch again; we talk every six to eight months, and I take him out on my expense account because I know I'm gonna do another story with the guy.

Then 9/11 happens. I call Vina. He's missing. I call his sister Carolyn. We all kind of knew, I think.

Mike asked me to do a videotape for Pat's memorial service, and as I was bonding with Mike, Bobby, Pat's best friend, and the guys at Ladder 3, I began to hear more Paddy Brown stories than I was aware of—about his life, and how deep it was, and how difficult some of it was, and how varied it was. And I said, "We gotta do something about this, Mike." So, after they found his body, and after we had another memorial service for him, we went to Hooters, of all places, and decided we were going to do something to memorialize him. And that became the film that I did, *Finding Paddy*, which was finding his life story.

Ninety-nine percent of firemen are guys like I grew up with. They grew up in the boroughs, or Long Island. They have kids, they have a family, they do their jobs, they go home, they retire after twenty, twenty-five years. You put on a uniform, you're gonna risk your life—so they are a different breed, there's no question about it. But most of them are "normal" guys. Pat was not a "normal" guy in that sense of the word. And I knew that from the first time I met him. In fact, in '91, when I was filming with FOX-TV, I was having dinner with Patrick, and a friend came to meet me, and Pat had to go to work. So we talked a bit, the three of us, and Pat left and my friend said, "What is behind that guy's eyes? What's goin' *on* in there?"

I think the thing about Patrick, number one, is that he was a superb, skilled leader. There's no question about that. He was a legend. He was an expert; he studied the art, the science of the whole firefighting thing. He was fearless. But what I also found out was that he was a true hero in the Greek sense of the word. That there are flaws in them, but they rise above those flaws. And *that's* what makes him a hero.

He had things happen in his life that caused him great suffering, which were not his fault—things that, because of alcoholism in his family, led him to go to Vietnam at an early age, which led him to being exposed to things that hurt him, which led him to come back to New York and basically do some crazy stuff—and then he became a fireman. He came to the realization that he then had to put the bottle down and try to heal himself from those traumas of his early life. To resurrect himself.

He was like a little kid looking through the glass at something he wanted, and that was a normal life, with a family and kids, and everything else. And with his face up against the glass, he just couldn't get it. But he was trying.

Vina Drennan said that he was like the knight in shining armor who would go through the dungeons and the swamps and the jungles, and fight the fights, but always come home to the family. And Pat was trying to complete that circle. He had gone and fought the battles, but he was going to try to come home and complete that circle. Have a normal life.

You (Sharon) were an important part of Paddy's healing, I think, and I hope that comes through in my film. Because he was trying to have a relationship that would eventually lead to marriage. He was really trying to do that with you. I think you said that he wasn't ready yet; his trauma wasn't healed yet, and that could have been true. I do think that in terms of his healing arc, that you were very significant. Because he had to try. You're the only one he asked to marry, at least that I know of, who all his family and friends know of, so that was a significant step in his healing process.

Every good story has an arc in it. After the early trauma, he actually began to heal himself— through running, boxing, karate, yoga, through trying relationships with women, through self-betterment, through diet— everything! He always strived to be a little better each day. And he was getting there. He never, ever stopped trying. If that's the only thing people take out of *Finding Paddy* I'd be thrilled. Don't give up.

BOBBY PERAZZO – Pat's Friend

I met Pat at my restaurant, Zinno's. First we became running partners, and then best friends. It must have been 1984 or '85; Pat and I had trained all year for the marathon and we thought we were gonna kick ass and do so well. It turned out that the day was kinda humid and a little warm. About midway through the race, somewhere on 1st Avenue, Pat started developing cramps in his legs, and couldn't rehydrate. And as anybody who runs knows, it was just god-awful, like the Death March from Bataan, just to get through the thing. After a while, he couldn't keep up and told me to just keep going. He was in so much pain that he could hardly move, and would stop at every firehouse on the route and have them massage his legs so he could plow through this thing. I waited for him at the end, and he finally appeared, after maybe five hours of extreme, extreme pain that he grueled through to finish this race. And then crawled home with us.

STEVE BAKER

Pat was my AA sponsor. I met him fifteen years ago through a mutual friend; he gave me his number and we started talking. I lived in Brooklyn and he lived in Manhattan. I'm not a fireman and I'm not an athlete; I like to eat and I'm a little round, and he respected me for who I am and didn't focus on what I'm not. Here I was, a Brooklyn guy, still living at home in my thirties, leading a very "neighborhood" life. He didn't judge me. Pat made me feel good about myself—like a man, an adult. And that's a "mensch," in a sense.

I don't really know about his fire department stuff; he never talked about it with me. But once he took me to a mass at St. Francis and I sat there with all these firemen, and I'm not even dressed.

And Pat says, "You're sittin' next to me." And people are like, oh, you're sittin' next to Patty Brown, you know, *"Patty Brown,"* like he's a rock star.

He called me his "little brother," and that's what I needed, because I came from a family where I was referred to as the drug addict, the ADD, always the wild one, always being abused, and I had all this shame-based low self-esteem and didn't understand what was going on here. Pat had a lot of adversity in his life, and he didn't want to see anyone else go through it without hope. Pat gave me strength. And he treated me like a brother. He also made me feel that he wanted to learn from me, which gave me a lot of self-respect.

He got me a book—I knew he was getting it for me, but I didn't want it—by Dr. Weil, because he wanted me to get healthy; he had a passion for health and spirituality. So I was two-hundred-and-sixty pounds at the time and wanted to lose weight.

And Pat goes, "Okay, you're gonna run fifteen minutes—no more, no less."

And I was running very slow, on the FDR Drive, and got to Waterside Plaza. I thought I was gonna die of a heart attack, I was so out of shape. And I see him riding that old bicycle of his, and he stopped and was so proud that I listened to him, that I did it. 'Cause I knew it was coming from Pat Brown. When Patty did something, he did it with conviction. He took the time to teach people. He loved to show you what he loved, and made you want to join in his passion. And I'm gonna do a marathon one day before I die—that's one of my goals.

Sometimes his passion could overwhelm. He told me a story how he almost got arrested for yelling at a vendor for charging too much money for coffee to a tourist. He didn't like people being taken advantage of. He was always for the underdog.

He hated racial intolerance. Just hated it. But he was diplomatic, because he had some friends who had prejudices. What was wonderful about Pat is that he had his beliefs, and he led by example.

Pat was a shy guy, insecure in some ways. He told me about his childhood; his childhood was tough. We shared things that a sponsor/sponsee would share. And he talked about anger. I didn't think I was an angry guy, because my issues were shame-based. But one day I got angry and he started laughing.

I said, "What?"

And he goes, "You finally got angry!" And he helped me to understand that you have to get it out, and deal with it.

We did have a falling out once—I was upset and didn't talk to him for six or seven months. But he did apologize, and I remember saying to him on September 9, 2001, "I'm happy you're back in my life." People are human. Patty Brown, too. And he always wanted to tell me he was human—that's the whole thing.

BOBBY PERAZZO

We all know about the "daring-do" stuff—I could go on and on about that. But there were some funny incidents.

Pat had come out to my house in East Hampton with a mutual friend, Jimmy G. They were both in AA; I was not. Jimmy had an AA friend who lived out there who was gonna meet us for a day at the beach. I had never met this gentleman before.

Some woman this guy was dating, also from AA, had just broken up with him, and he was out of his mind with anger and grief—you know, "the women of the world are so terrible," and "she's probably a lesbian," and on and on—and Pat just rolled his eyes and kinda walked away. After an hour of that, we piled into our car and went to town for breakfast. Pat and I just kinda looked at each other as he continued ranting and had our breakfast separately. Then we all went to the beach. Jimmy passes out on the blanket. This guy is going on, with Pat, still venting about this girl, and I say, "I'm goin' running."

I come back forty-five minutes later and can see Pat, kind of sitting on the blanket, moving back and forth, really agitated. And I'm getting closer and can still see this guy jabberin' away, amazingly, *still* about this girl. I get up to the blanket as Pat finally turns to him and says, "My advice is—get a .38. Put two bullets in it. Shoot her first, and think about shooting yourself."

"Success is to be measured not so much by the position that one has reached in life as by the obstacles which he has overcome while trying to succeed." —Booker T. Washington

Journal Entry – February 26, 2004

At last, a warm tease is in the air. The river ice is breaking up yet still clings to the banks with a late February stubbornness, a warning not to put away those mittens just yet. The center is flat and reflects a slate sky with cirrus smudged around the bright sun.

Riding into the city in the late afternoon, I plan to meet Frank, Pat's childhood friend, whom I first encountered over two years ago at Frank E. Campbell's Funeral Home. The notion that a boyhood pal existed, to whom I could talk and discover the source waters of what had flowed in the man, was an unanticipated gift.

The occasion had been the second memorial service for Pat, almost two months after the profoundly moving and traffic-stopping service held on his forty-ninth birthday at St. Patrick's Cathedral. This time with a casket and the all-too-physical and all-too-sacred remains. I was unnerved with the fear that he was in pieces, just on the other side of the flag-draped coffin. Somehow, it was far easier to imagine he had vaporized, instantly becoming one with the universe, a spirit in the skies and in our hearts, when no remains had been found. But in mid- December, the discovery was made, and I chose to ask nothing of details. I can't bear them, the indication that he suffered. That strong body that I knew so well, broken and cold.

But meeting Frank was a door opening, and we were off this evening to find Suspenders, the downtown branch of the bar that Pat and many other off-duty firefighters called home in the 1980s, when drink and drugs and sex were the wallpaper of New York City nightlife.

Frank and I drove down lower Broadway, on one of the very few occasions that I have been below Canal Street since 9/11. We kept our gazes level with the street, looking for the entrance of Suspenders, looking for a parking spot, and looking anywhere but up into the void where the towers once stood. The missing frame of reference left nothing to denote direction headed or distance traveled, and the physical disorientation seemed emotionally apt.

As we finally descended the steps that led to the bar, the wall of noise told me I was not going to have a few hours of quiet, intimate reminiscing by fellow co-workers, fondly remembering Patty Brown with the friendly smile and big moustache and boxer's fast hands, ready to bounce any trouble out of the premises should his charm not be sufficient.

A farewell party was going on for a bartender, and the bar crowd was caught in the alcohol-infused loop of forced gaiety and decompression after one business day ends and before the next begins.

The very dapper and genial owner, Billy Ahearn, came over and introduced himself. Against the din, he shared some recollections about Pat. We lamented 9/11 in a way that didn't require elaboration. Billy had his FDNY career during the 1970s, the "war years," and was practiced in the art of loss. Still, all that practice could not prepare any of them for the loss of 343, including the very best of the best, in one fell swoop.

I asked if I could return at a quieter time, before Wall Street's closing bell perhaps, when he might share some more. By now the background karaoke was well into the foreground, approaching torturous levels. One bond trader, his tie still snug in his Brooks Brothers collar, picked up the mike and unbelievably, broke off-key into Bruce Springsteen's "The

Rising." I didn't know whether to laugh or cry.

BILLY AHEARN – Owner of Suspenders Bar in Lower Manhattan
Larry Fitzpatrick was probably my best friend in life; he was a firefighter
killed in 1980. He was a Harlem firefighter and owned a bar on 38th
Street. I used to work for him there; I was the doorman.

He came in one day and said, "Billy, we got a great probie, got this kid
Patty Brown. He ain't much to look at." He said, "The kid's wonderful." So
he introduced me to Pat, and I got to know him quite a bit, and you know
you think you know people and then you really don't, because Pat was one
of those true heroes in life—who don't tell you what they do; they do it.

So I spoke to him at length about Vietnam. I went to Vietnam as a kid,
but I didn't go as a soldier, I used to bring in munitions. I used to see quite
a bit of, uh…nonsense over there, and I would speak to him, and at no
time in the conversation did he ever tell me he had a Silver Star—'cause
that's not what he was about. And he was like that in the fire department,
too. And I'm fortunate in my life to see and firsthand witness people who
are the true heroes, you know, few and far between do we use that term.
But Pat was, and what always struck me is that every conversation I ever
had with him, it was never "him" in the conversation; it wasn't what "he
did;" it was quite the opposite. You had to drag it out of him.

I did martial arts as a kid; he was into martial arts, and I talked to him
a number of conversations. He didn't tell me he was teaching the blind,
he'd tell me he's "working out."

You know, "So what are you doing now?"

"Eh, I'm workin' out." That was it.

At Suspenders, we made him a bouncer, and everybody kept saying
that's an awful small bouncer, and I said there's a reason we made him a
bouncer; we're not paying him here because he's one-hundred and sixty
pounds. But what he *does* with this… We had a football team smoker, and
to generate money we'd bring in some fighters, and Patty would come in
and always do us a favor, and he would only be as good as the guy in the

ring; he was never there to embarrass anybody or hurt anybody. And depending on the caliber of the guy he was fighting, that's what he would do. And he never beat anybody up; I really tipped my hat to him on that. One fellow came up to us afterward, complaining: "You put me in there with a pro!" And I said, "Yeah, and he did a pro job; he didn't beat up on you. Otherwise we wouldn't be having this conversation!"

He was working out at Gleason's and whatnot; he was an accomplished boxer. Another thing you'd never know about him; he wouldn't say that. He was an accomplished man in the martial arts, boxing, firefighting, the Marines, everything—the top of his game in everything, and he never told you about it.

MIKE SHEPHERD – Squad 41, FDNY, and former *Daily News* Golden Gloves Champion
He'd watch me box in the gym, and up 'til the day he got killed in 9/11, he always wanted to come sparrin' with me at Gleason's. He was an older guy and a lot lighter. He had more heart than anything. Ya know what I'm sayin'? What he had in heart, if he was eight feet tall, he coulda conquered the world.

MIKE McPARLAND – Battalion Chief, FDNY
I first met Patty about 1980. We worked at Suspenders together. He was either the doorman and I was the bar boy, or he was the bartender, or I was the bartender and he was the bar boy; anyway, we were in that whole circuit of workin' down there.

I always got a kick out of him, 'cause he'd jump on his bike or he'd jog all the way to Rescue 2 from Manhattan to Brooklyn.

"Eh, no problem." Off he went.

A couple late nights we bartended together, and I wasn't able to make it home. I went over to his apartment, and I don't know how many cats he had, but it was like *Wild Kingdom*—there was animals all over the place.

I said, "Patty, you're killin' me." He had cats, he had this, he had that, he had a ferret…so he was a big nature lover. Who knew? He was a mysterious guy in a lotta ways.

One night Patty was workin' the door, and Patty wasn't a big guy. And there was a wise guy, 6'2" or so, and he said something; I think he took a swing at Patty. And one shot, the guy was on the floor; he was out.

I go, "Whoa! What happened?"

And he says, "C'mon, Mike, gimme a hand with this guy." So we pulled him outside and put him on the sidewalk. You'd never think he was a boxer. All he said was, "Yeah, I was on the Marine Corps boxing team." Just lookin' at him, you'd never think he was the way he was. Soft-spoken, never got excited. Super guy. He was the real deal.

BRUCE SILVERGLADE – Owner of Gleason's Gym

I first met Pat when Gleason's was located in Manhattan on the corner of 30th and Eighth, and he was a regular. I knew him for a good twenty years. Pat was a real hardworking individual, dedicated to what he did, certainly on the job, and he was the same way in the gym. Gleason's Gym is unique, it's a specialist gym; it's a fight gym. So we only have good fighters and good amateurs and pros.

Back in the days when Pat was there, we had very few business people, so when Pat came in, he actually worked hard with the pros. He was in the ring sparring with people like Roberto Duran, who was one of our great all-time champions. Pat was in the gym probably when Mohammed Ali was still coming, toward the end of his career. Pat would spar with anybody. Fearless, he went into the ring to spar for training, and to help the fighters prepare for their fights, as a fighter. He did not go in there to pitty-pat or to say, "Let's just move around, and take it easy with me." I know that he was also in the ring with Jerry Cooney, who was a much bigger person than him, but that's the kind of guy that Pat was. He went in there to actually compete. He was a good defensive fighter; he was a strong fellow so he had a good punch, and there was nobody that he was afraid of.

When he came in, we'd talk a little about what was going on in his job, because it was always interesting to me. Every now and then, he'd tell me about some heroic deed that he was involved with; however, he never bragged or put himself in the limelight. He took as second nature what I and most people wouldn't dream of doing. He'd say, "Hey, this is my job—this is what I do," and he went and did it very efficiently. And in the gym, he was just one of the guys, one of the boxers. Very, very well-liked.

We always have had world champions, so if Roberto Duran is here, or Mohammed Ali is here, or Mike Tyson is here—for me, that's business, that's normal. It's not as exciting as it is to see a real-life hero come in, and talk to somebody like that. Pat was a legitimate hero. It was exciting to have him here.

HECTOR ROCA — Trainer at Gleason's Gym

I was still a new trainer at Gleason's, and I see him spar with Roberto Duran. I say, "Who's this guy?" I think he's a professional fighter, and they say, "No, he's a fireman." And I say, "Oh, he's good!"

Early mornings, he rides his bicycle here to work out. He never took a trainer; he like to come and work out by himself. Sometimes I help him tie his glove, but that's it.

He like to spar with professionals. He's a tough guy—lots of moves, lots of combinations. But he's very humble; he get along with everybody, and people like him when he come in here.

One time he go to Panama. The fire department sent people to Central America for seminars to help fire departments there. I'm from Panama, so we talk. He say he enjoy it, it's beautiful, he like it.

He look like Burt Reynolds, with a big moustache.

I feel so bad, because he's a nice guy. Good heart. A big, big loss for New York. But good people stay in your heart.

GEORGE MENAR — Former Fire Patrolman

One day, I was at the Fire Patrol house, and Patty comes bustin' in the

door. I thought he had just got mugged—all messed up, blood comin'
out...

I said, "What the hell happened to you?"

He goes, "George, this is the greatest day of my life!"

I go, "*What?* You look like you just got hit by a train!"

"No—it was three rounds with Roberto Duran."

I said, "You are nuts, Patty."

BOB JACKSON – Trainer at Gleason's Gym

I was a sergeant in the Corrections Department and had started a boxing
club at Sing Sing. I used to bring the amateurs from the street into the
prison to box the prisoners. And it was all straight up and down—the
prisoners were licensed with the USA Boxing Association. The Police
Department boxers didn't wanna come, didn't wanna hear the catcalls and
boos. I said, once the fight starts, it'll simply be fight fans. So I asked
about bringing the Fire Department team instead. We brought them up,
and Pat was on the team.

Pat's match was with a big guy doing twenty-five-to-life for murder,
and he said to me, "What are you doin', putting me in with a killer?"

I said, "What do you care what he did? All that matters is what he can
do in the ring, right?" And they had a *hell* of a fight. Pat lost the decision,
but he was nice enough to admit that it wasn't a hometown decision. If
they didn't win, they didn't get it. Whoever won got it. But it was a very,
very hard fight. The prisoner won by just a hair. And after the fight, what
we used to do is have a chicken dinner, the prisoners along with the guys
they fought. We'd fill up one big mess hall. And Pat sat and ate with the
guy who beat him.

A little later, that guy saw in the newspaper the roof rope rescue that
Pat led, and wrote me a letter: "Sarge! I fought a Hero!" and he enclosed
the photo from the news. "Tell Pat I said Wow, I'm so glad they didn't fall,
and so happy for him, and thank god he's okay!" When I told Pat, he was
touched. I gave him the letter. The prisoner's name was "Spider" Freeman.

Far as I know, he's still doing that time.

I think a lot of good came out of the boxing—giving guys discipline to use in life. Sometimes you do something with the intent that this will be a good thing, trying to get people to respect themselves and others. And when you have that view, hoping for a ripple effect, there's also the big overview that turns into something like Pat. But Pat...Pat was Pat.

"If your actions inspire others to dream more, learn more, do more and become more, you are a leader." —JOHN QUINCY ADAMS

Journal Entry – March 2, 2004

A dentist appointment and some errands had me in the Ladder 3 neighborhood, just south of Union Square. In the latter part of the last millennium, Captain Pat Brown didn't have a firehouse to call his own. He was unceremoniously bounced around, filling vacancies temporarily, yet hoping to land the captaincy in this tough, old, legendary firehouse.

Originating on September 11, 1865, near the conception of the FDNY, Ladder Company 3 has housed its truck in the old brick building on E.13th Street since 1929. The fact that it does not share its space with an Engine gives "3 Truck" the leeway to race out to any fire within its jurisdiction and hook up with the first Engine on the scene. It is aggressive and elite, and hasn't slowed down much despite the fact that the neighborhood has evolved from being among the most dangerous (the famous final shoot-out in the movie *Taxi Driver* took place just down the street, reflecting the 1970s real-life scene) to now safely housing an NYU dorm and plenty of yoga studios.

In 2000 Pat settled in and found it to be a perfect fit with his new, quieter lifestyle. He was within eight blocks in either direction of his home in StuyvesantTown, and his home away from home, Jivamukti Yoga Center. "Uptown Patty Brown" was settling down. He provided a teak bench for the sidewalk outside the watch area and took his deli coffee and *Daily News* to sit there, watching his city go by.

MIKE SHEPHERD

He didn't wanna be livin' out of a friggin' suitcase, you know, bouncin' from Brooklyn to Queens to Staten Island. You wanna know you have a place—I go there, I'm the Captain, that's it. Three Truck was perfect for Patty. And he had great guys, he had hard-chargin' guys. And they were the *biggest* guys in the fire department. And they loved Patty. They woulda followed him anywhere.

They knew his reputation when he came there, and they were a little worried. Because he didn't drink, you know; he wasn't into partyin'. And they didn't know how he would take them, if he was gonna be a freakin' reformer. But Patty gave it to them: "Let's just go to fires, and let's not get into trouble." Then he gets these two-hundred-and-seventy-five-pound guys doin' yoga.

JACK JANSEN – Fire Chief, Columbia, South Carolina, Retired
I first met Paddy at the quarters of Engine 277 in Brooklyn, about 1968. He was about sixteen, an Explorer riding with the Engine with a covering lieutenant from Queens Village for the day. His face shone with interest and amazement at the things he saw and heard while around the FDNY. He was a handsome, wide-eyed boy, basking in the grownup world of fire-fighters, and he loved every minute.

I saw myself in him that day; I could tell that he, like myself, was hooked on wanting to become a firefighter. It was the beginning of a long friendship, not as close as I would have liked it to be. We did run around together, "buffing" fires for several years.

As he got older, we would run into each other many times. I remember his frustration at having to wait years to get on the job. I remember the hard years during Vietnam and after, and I especially remember his elation at getting on the FDNY. He took to it like a fish takes to water, and gave the FDNY, the city, and the citizens more than any one man had given before. I watched his antics on TV and told people, "I know him!" He made everyone who knew him proud.

The last time I saw him was in 1999. Both of us had gotten a little older, and we talked about how long we could go in this business. We laughed about possibly being buried in the firehouse garden so we wouldn't be far from the smoke and flames. When I left the firehouse that night, I still detected a bit of that wide-eyed boy in my friend of thirty-one years. Little did I know we would never meet again in this world.

Journal Entry – October 4, 2001

Pat's car is still parked on the street in front of the firehouse, almost a month after he drove to work that last morning he reported for duty. Someone had tucked a single yellow rose under the windshield wiper. A sweet and sad boutonniere for the last dance of an old Honda Civic.

TIM GUINEE – Pat's Friend

I was down at the firehouse, and they got this run. He asked me if I wanted to ride along, so I went. It was a person trapped under a subway car. I remember Patty was giving instructions to a probie, and saying, "No matter what, don't go down under the train," because of the electricity I guess, on the third rail. If you have a fatality, they just shut the line down so there's no current running under there, and then deal with getting the body out.

When we got to the subway station, it turned out that the guy was alive under the train, and I think he had lost a leg. But he was alive and trapped. Patty immediately discarded his own advice and went down under the train and got the guy out. Didn't wait for anybody to turn off the electric. Or anything like that. Which was pretty extraordinary. And then didn't really have anything to say about it. It was just work.

Around 9/11, all the conversation involved calling people "hero this" and "hero that." I think that the word is so overused in our vernacular. It has this kind of strange meaning that connotes a kind of super-human, beyond the pale of what normal people are like. And what's truly extraordinary about Pat, about heroic people, is that they're people. He certainly was a guy who had his challenges and his demons, but he was kind of blessed in other areas. In his ability to respond to situations like that. On a level, I think some people are heroic *because* they are human beings, *because* they're flawed like everybody.

I remember sitting on the bench outside the firehouse, Pat talking about some heavy stuff——military things that had gone on, and places in his life that were tough. And across the street there's this dormitory and these NYU college girls started dancing in the window, and all the guys in the firehouse came out and stood there and watched. It almost felt like some kind of weird, hilarious nightly ritual. And he had a great sense of humor about that. Just the fact that a guy walks into a firehouse with a yoga mat rolled up under his arm, you know, takes a certain self-assurance.

The other thing with Patty was that he made you want to be good by example. He sort of did the right thing, or was struggling to do the right thing, and that kind of modesty you wanted to emulate. You wanted to create ripples in the world that were as positive as the ones he created through his actions.

So 9/11 happened, and it twisted my head around, like so many people. The *Ladder 49* movie came along, and I really wanted to do it as a tribute to Patty, and to firefighters in general. I had some pictures of Patty on the set with me. I talked to the guys a lot about 9/11, and just wanted to make sure there was a sense of gravity to what we were doing, and not just making some dumb movie (and, to be fair to the other actors, they were pretty aware of that).

As part of the training for the movie, they put us all through the Academy and farmed us out to various fire stations throughout the city, Baltimore, where we would ride along and go in working fires, and work with the guys and do everything. There was a fire in a fourteen-story tenement building, and the standpipes were shut down so no water could get up. And it was rolling pretty good up there. I wound up finding this woman and getting her out. I mean, I practically tripped over her; it was kind of a lucky thing. Certainly, when you compare it to the stuff Patty did, it's just silly. But I'm happy that whatever tiny bits of good I can do in some way came out of Patty. The impulse to do that movie came out of knowing Patty. And the intensity of the work to get it right came out of knowing Patty. And being in that fire and finding that woman there came out of Patty. And my joining the VFD, subsequent to that. Those are all results of seeing somebody do the right thing, and trying to do the right thing yourself. And I'm a lousy fireman! I mean, to even talk about being a fireman in the same breath as you talk about Patty Brown being a fireman is ludicrous. I'm just a struggling new guy trying to learn what I can learn. But sometimes I get to help the department do good, and that's because of Patty.

BILLY AHEARN

There's a difference in leadership. You can push or you can pull—Pat pulled. He'd go do it, so guys would say, "I'm gonna do what he's doin'." He was good enough to impart to men that they can't do everything he does. Out of ten thousand firemen, five of them are just on a different level. Everybody's good in the New York City Fire Department, nobody's bad, believe me, they're the finest in the world; they pride themselves on that. Then there're those guys that are—BONG! They just have something else the rest of us don't have. And when they become lieutenants and captains, they go in and do these death-defying things. Patty was one of them.

"What man actually needs is not a tensionless state but rather the striving and struggling for some goal worthy of him. What he needs is not the discharge of tension at any cost, but the call of a potential meaning waiting to be fulfilled by him." ——Victor Frankl

Journal Entry – March 11, 2004

I am trying to think what to say when Steve McCarthy asks me with his camera rolling for his documentary, "So how did you and Pat meet?"

Technically, we met earlier, after the Watts Street fire. But for me it really began differently, more symbolically, a little later. In more ways than one, I did not know who Pat Brown was. When he introduced himself to me, I had a blindfold on. Literally.

His first words were: "You're doing great, Senpai. It's Pat."

And I thought, Pat? Pat who?

On a Wednesday evening in October 1995, he was guiding me and other students through a karate class at the Blind Association on 23rd Street. Our school, Seido Karate, runs the program for blind and vision-impaired students, and part of promotion to the next black belt level would always include joining in this class. Throwing a roundhouse kick, executing a kata, or blocking an opponent you can't even see is very disorienting and sometimes frightening if you normally rely on your vision. Thus we are humbled and appreciate what we take for granted on a day-to-day basis.

The students Pat helped every week had no blindfold to take off at the end of class. With what I imagine was the same calm assurance and support I felt at my elbow that evening, Pat Brown really entered my peripheral vision. He constantly over the years encouraged his students, whose obstacles were so much greater than mine.

ROXANNE BEBEE BLATZ – Sensei at Seido Karate
Pat meant a lot to the Seido Blind and Visually Impaired Program. The students loved him, and he actually believed in them. Too many people go into helping people with impairments and instead of encouraging them, they patronize them. Pat could be tough on the students, but he was also compassionate. He pushed them hard to be the best they could be. He listened to their stories and gave them hope.

He helped our student Nooria very much when someone slammed her to the floor of a subway platform and smashed her face with a brick. This caused Nooria to have a further loss of sight and sent her into despair. She was thinking about quitting karate, and Pat talked to her and encouraged her to continue. He told her she was strong and that she couldn't let the other person win and control her life.

Pat was so modest. I will never forget on the day he got his Nidan (second-degree black belt); as he was coming through the line, he hugged me for what seemed like forever and whispered, "Sensei Roxanne, one of my true heroes." He always gave Sensei Paul and me a lot of credit for our dedication to the Seido Blind and Visually Impaired Program, and he always downplayed his role. But it was significant.

NOORIA NODRAT – Student at Seido Karate and NYC College of Technology
I am originally from Afghanistan. I came to the U.S. in 1991, a year after I lost my husband to a terrorist bomb. I was vision-impaired, and so went to the Catholic Guild for the Blind to learn English. From there I was sent to the Associated Blind on 23rd Street, which provides different activities

for vision-impaired and blind people. I registered, and one of my classes was karate.

In my third class, I met Senpai Brown. He was a very, very attractive man, a tall and handsome "karate guy," and I thought, Wow, I don't know if I can learn from him. But he was a wonderful person inside—a very kind, generous, and patient instructor.

Along with still learning English, I also had to learn the Japanese for the karate techniques. It was quite a challenge, not only for me, but for my senpais. They had to show me what is "palm," for instance, in English, then also in Japanese. They had to let us touch each part of their hands, their legs, their movements, their kicks… For us to have the right technique we need to feel it, to touch it, and they were willing to do that for us.

I was going for my green belt promotion. Besides doing the physical part, we also have to write an essay about what karate means to us. Senpai Brown was helping me to write my essay as I dictated to him.

I told him about what happened, how I lost my sight. I started crying because it was the first time that somebody allowed me to express my feelings about my injury. It wasn't nature that brought me into this position. A sick person attacked me and caused me to lose my sight completely. I was very depressed in the beginning, and I was afraid. As if I might put one step in front of me and fall into a big hole.

Senpai Brown gave me a hug and held me and told me, "It's okay, Nooria. Cry if you want to. Let it go." And then he told me after a while, "You're the same Nooria you used to be. Look inside of you and you will discover yourself. Blindness is just one part of you; you still breathe, you eat, you do your regular things, and I am sure you will accomplish a lot in your life." Then he told me, "If you fall down seven times, get up eight. Never give up, and always try again. Even if you fall many times."

I learned so much from him. Not just karate techniques. I learned discipline, dignity, respect for myself as well as others. He taught me, don't ever let myself go down and say "Okay, Destiny, you can take me wherever you want to take me." I have to change my destiny to my own favor.

Author's Note

Nooria was the first person I sought for my story collection. My detective skills were still in an embryonic stage, and I knew neither her last name nor her whereabouts after 9/11. I tried, but I could not find her after she took Pat's advice and seized the wheel to her own destiny. Then, the day after the 2006 New York marathon, my eye caught an article about a blind woman running in it:

ASSOCIATED PRESS – November 5, 2006

Nooria Nodrat's legs and hands went numb in the 24th mile in the New York City Marathon on Sunday. So she rested for half an hour before finishing. The 45-year-old Nodrat ran and walked the course through the city's five boroughs tethered to a rotating team of supporters with a dish towel. She finished in about seven hours. "I want to continue my running until the age of 90," she said, undeterred by the numbness, which she thought might have had to do with hunger or her asthma. "Every year I want a marathon."

Training for the marathon, Nodrat said, helped lift her out of the depression that enveloped her after she lost her sight. She was inspired by her older brother, Zia, who despite his own blindness studied for two college degrees before being executed by Islamic extremists, she said. Because of her devotion to him, Nodrat learned Braille as a teenager, years before the knowledge would help in her own life. She hopes eventually to help blind women and children in Afghanistan, where "they think [the blind] are not worthy," Nodrat said. "I realized blindness is not the end of life. It's a part of life but it's not the end of my life. I am still a human being and I have to go on. And I'm fine with my blindness now," she said.

SANDRA RANDALL – Nidan, Seido Blind and Visually Impaired Program

Pat was the only instructor who was willing to work with me on my terms. Other instructors kept to the rules, like "I tell you to do this and you do it." No interaction. And he wasn't like that. He called me "Buddy."

"What's the matter, Buddy? What's the problem?"

I said, "Pat, I can't work this way," because when you're totally blind, *space* is your enemy. You have to give me an idea; what are the surroundings? So that when you tell me to make a ninety-degree or a one-hundred-and-eighty-degree or whatever, then I know where I am, where I have to go, so that I can do it again. What the other instructors do—they always place you, turn you to where you need to go, and I said, "That's no good."

So Pat said, "Well, what can I do to help you?" And he was willing to do that.

When I did kata, it's very important to go in the right direction, you know, so he'd say, "The stage is in the front—now *go*," and that way he didn't have to place me. Sometimes he'd adjust me a little, but that's how I learned to do kata. Your muscles learn—muscle memory. And that was how I learned, because he was willing to not be so orthodox.

He invited me to lunch a couple of times, but every time he did, I was always on the move; I was busy. "Aw, come on and have lunch," he says, "I'm payin'!" But he was always that way. He'd see me on the street: "Hey, Sandra! What's up? How you doin'?" He would always stop and say hello.

I knew him for at least five years. He was studying to become a chief in the FDNY. The amazing thing was—he worked all day or would work all night, then come here. A lot of times he was in pain; he'd say his back was killing him. But he would still come, and always cheerful, too—he never moaned and groaned. He was always "up." It wasn't an unpleasant task for him. And teaching blind people is not easy.

Sometimes he would say, "Now how can I show you this? This is hard to describe, Sandra. Maybe I can show you—hold onto my hand, and I can show you." And he did a good job. And he was willing to work with the totally blind. It is frustrating to a sighted person to teach a totally blind person—very, very hard.

He wouldn't let me give up either. I'd say, "I can't do it."

He'd say, "Oh, yes you can." Would *not* let you give up.

Village Voice — Alisa Solomon — September, 2001

Karate Grandmaster Kaicho Nakamura opened his mail on Thursday to find a donation and a note of support, dated September 10, for an upcoming benefit tournament from one of his senior students, Patrick Brown. The generosity didn't surprise Nakamura; Brown always looks for ways to contribute and help others. A second-degree black belt, Brown, 48, is more widely known as the most highly decorated captain in the New York Fire Department. He dashed into the debris-laden cloud at the Twin Towers on Tuesday, along with his brothers from Ladder Co. 3, just before the first tower crumbled. "He is a true hero," Nakamura said.

It's a title Brown earned over and over, but he would brush it off whenever any of his fellow students at Seido Karate expressed admiration for the many daring rescues he performed. A quiet man with smiling blue eyes, Brown "never once praised himself or gave himself credit," said his good friend and training buddy, Ralph Palmieri. He'd even be a little timid in sparring, Palmieri adds, concerned that he might hurt someone. The two served together as volunteers at Seido's karate program for blind students, and Brown would tell Palmieri, "Those students are the real heroes."

For the last eight years, Palmieri and Brown had sushi lunches three times a week after karate class. When not joined by others, Brown would bring up another area where he and Palmieri shared deep feelings: their service in Vietnam. Brown had been in the Marines, Palmieri in the Army.

"He'd talk about how bad he felt about all the bad things that happened over there, and how he hoped he could do enough good to make up for it," Palmieri said. "I am sure his score is settled."

KAICHO TADASHI NAKAMURA — Grandmaster, World Seido Karate

"Ko In Ya No Gotoshi." (Japanese translation for "time flies")

Sensei Patrick Brown is a Seido hero, not because of his black belt rank, but because of his strong determination and the way he cared for people. For me, these were his outstanding qualities.

Personally, I appreciate the fact that he chose Seido from so many alternative martial- art systems and schools. Since my philosophy is to treat all my students equally, I never treated him like a special person. That's why I believe he liked Seido. His training was steady, and Patrick showed true dedication to the martial arts, always with Bushido spirit.

I didn't know that he was a captain in the New York City Fire Department, nor that he was a decorated Vietnam War hero. He was very quiet, with a humble demeanor. He never drew attention to himself. He never asked for help, but rather, he always asked what *he* could do to help. That was the spirit I came to know in Patrick Brown, my student.

He was not only a strong karate-ka, but he also had a samurai spirit. He would not show pain, but just kept it to himself. He did not want to worry people with his difficulties or pain. On the contrary, he tried to absorb other people's pain——*he* took it. I am sure that during his time on this earth, he experienced hell many times, on the battlefield or in a burning building. If he hadn't had those experiences, he might have been more easy-going and openly sought pleasure. He was always serious and trying to help people——that was the quality of his life.

Quite often he attended Friday afternoon meditation class. He would always sit still, grounded, with a very strong focus. He would always focus his gaze on me as I spoke, listening intently, almost like he was trying to bite and chew on the words.

I regret that I could not have been closer to him. Perhaps Patrick would have allowed me to help or lessen his pain. Everybody who met him would say, "Patrick is such a nice person." As a human being, with outstanding qualities, he also sometimes needed an outlet, or a way to express his feelings. As his instructor, I believe that by training at karate, he could provide some rest for his spirit.

Our lives are accumulations of moments—how we dedicate ourselves and appreciate what we have. The way Pat lived, the way he died—tell us of his responsibility, the way he cared for people, his passion, everything. Even on September 11th, in the hell that must have been the tower, he didn't turn back. That kind of spirit is really, really remarkable.

So many people miss, appreciate, admire Pat. I appreciate his giving us so many lessons by the way he lived, providing a kind of guidance to us, his friends. We have to appreciate all he's done. I believe he's always watching us.

PAT BROWN *—Men's Journal:* "The Lure of Danger," – April, 1998 (Cover Story by Sebastian Junger)

"I've always reacted well under intense, insane circumstances. Keeping calm and doing the right thing, maybe being very violent when the time came; just being able to react. I mean, a lot of people, they sort of get stunned for a second, like a deer in the headlights. I've never had that problem. I just feel like I'm in a zone, you know? The Japanese would say you're empty. You know what I mean? Empty but ready and full of thoughts."

THOMAS VON ESSEN – Former Commissioner, FDNY

The thing that amazed me about Pat was the different kind of courage he had to face people who don't have the best interest of the department at heart. What was so powerful about Pat is the fact that he really, really cared what people—people who had that type of courage, and I'll put myself in that category—thought of him or his performance. Yet he couldn't care at all—at *all*—what the "users" thought about him. And the department has lots of users—the people who walk around with their chests out, taking credit for the attitude and the spirit and the performance of the Browns, the Hattons, the Downeys, and on and on and on. These guys set that bar, and we all try to reach it. And when you get a chance to work with a Patty Brown, you want to take that honesty, that intensity, that pride that they bring. You want to take it, and you want to get it everywhere, and you know you can't. You get guys like him—wherever he goes, he's gonna raise it up a notch. If it's already at a high level, he's gonna take it to the next level. You could never raise the bar if it wasn't for a guy like Patty, or so many guys who were willing to step up and help me. But boy, he was one of them.

People think that everybody at the department is concerned about the good of the department. That just isn't the way it is. It's no different from any other organization. You have twelve thousand people, and out of that you have many hairbags you wish you could fire, and when you go after them, they become your enemies. And they're at every rank. The Patty Browns of the world had no patience for and would not suffer them.

There was a fire over on the East River, Waterside Towers in April, 2001; we had a really tough job there, and it was blowin' out some of those windows. I always tried to go up because I wanted to see how tough a job it was and what a good job they did or whatever; of course, most of the time they had already *done* the job. Patty came down, all full of soot, and he was telling us how helpful the thermal-imaging cameras were. Lynn Tierney said, "God, let's get him over to the TV people!" because he was such a great spokesperson—I mean, he was in shape, he was good-looking, he was well-spoken, he had balls like a lion. He just couldn't wait to tell everybody how good this product was and how it helped him help the guys that day. It made a difference because if he wasn't able to pinpoint the fire as fast as he did, who knows if it would've gotten above them or trapped them? He was so supportive of—in a rational way and in an intelligent way—all the stuff we were trying to do, and had no problem at all telling you if he disagreed with a particular thing, which wasn't very often because he knew that everything we were trying to do was for the good of the department. And he just appreciated that. He had never seen it before; he had never seen people who cared so much about safety and affecting change. I mean, he had no interest in coming down and being part of the suits that were trying to effectuate that change. But he certainly was a supporter in the field, arguing with people all the time, trying to get them to do their jobs. I remember going through this battle with him all the time (and you'd have the same battle with all the really good guys)—they would always be trying to get the best guys for their company. Like Steinbrenner, they wanted the five best guys, so that when they went out that door, they knew those five would be able to do a superior job in taking care of each other and taking care of their responsibility to the citizens.

He was always trying to help me do my job, and it looked like he was more interested in globally helping the department as he got older. He would've been a great chief, but I guess he had no interest in being a battalion chief. Guys like Pat feel like they can do the most at the captain's level, and they're right. I think the battalion chief is the most important job in the department, but the captain's is the hardest.

NY Daily News – April 24, 2001

FDNY officials credited a new heat-spotting camera with helping to save lives. Firefighters in the smoke-filled hallways used the device, which they had received the day before, to direct water toward flames they couldn't see.

The first wave of firefighters rode up to the blaze in an elevator. Confronted with black smoke and hot spots of more than 1,000 degrees, they used a thermal camera to spot a ceiling of flame above them.

"You get nervous," said Capt. Patrick Brown, one of the first firefighters at the scene.

"You're scared, and you've only got five minutes of air left in your tank."

PAT BROWN

I never knew it was that dangerous. (Laughter.) At least now I know.

DONALD HAYDE – Battalion Chief, FDNY

He was always in the right place at the right time. The fire would always kinda find him.

Sports Illustrated – December, 2001

Patty Brown…was a fire department legend: a man-about-town and one of the best firefighters in the city. One night in his life is now part of his legacy. There was a big fire in a West Side brownstone with a massive mahogany front door. Before the responding firefighters…even had a chance to size up the situation, the front door popped open from the inside. Out walked Patty Brown, wearing a suit and a tie, with an elderly man, unharmed, draped over his shoulder. Brown happened to have been down the block, on a dinner date, when he saw smoke. That was his knack, to be at the right place at the right time…

LOUIS GARCIA – Chief Fire Marshal, FDNY

Things would always happen to Patty. He could be walkin' down the street, and if someone was gonna jump, he'd jump in front of Pat. He got involved with more robberies, more jumpers, more fires—just by running around Manhattan. He used to get involved in everything. He didn't avoid situations.

Pat and I were bouncers at Suspenders together, 1979 to '80. He was a skinny kid, but nobody doubted he could handle himself, 'cause he had that look—that Charles Bronson look. And he was intense.

He also had the hero-look, demeanor, the whole aura. People were impressed. He had something in him that attracted people to him. And people loved to say his name—Patty Brown, Patty Brown, Patty Brown.

I remember seeing him at a big fire we were investigating at Waterside Towers. So there's Pat at the fire—I think he made a rescue or somethin'; somethin' big happened.

So he comes out of the building: "Hey, Louis! How're you doin'?"

I look at him and say, "What're you, a fuckin' hero again? I mean, what happened?" And if you look at Pat, with his dirty face and everything, I'm sayin' to myself, This is, like, made for the news. He's *made* to be in the newspaper. And I'm laughin' to myself, Oh, of course! It's Patty Brown, Patty Brown, Patty Brown! You just mention his name and people associate some heroic deed to it.

He was genuine. And you could kid around with him. I was also impressed by the diversity of his friends—black, white, gay, straight—and he was not ashamed to have anyone associated with him. Most firefighters stay with their mostly Irish-Catholic roots—Pat was the furthest thing from that. And that's something that was unique about Pat, in the context of the firefighter world, especially at that time. He was not judgmental. And he was never at a loss for a date.

Pat inspired people. Men genuinely liked him; even the ones who may have been jealous had to like him. He lived his work.

RICK SERRENTINO – NYPD Detective, Retired

It was 1984. I had just become a cop and had not even hit the streets yet. One night, after orientation, a group of us went out for drinks at a bar called Suspenders, where I was introduced to Patty. In those days he was still drinking. He looked at me and said, "Hey, I like cops. I almost became a cop." We laughed, had a few beers, and I went home.

The next day was my first day out on actual patrol. I was working out of the Midtown South precinct, which covers Times Square. After roll call, I got my radio and walked out to my post—42nd Street and 8th Avenue. I didn't even make it a block when I saw a huge crowd in the street, and people waving for me to come over. I was scared shitless! For the first time ever, I was going to act as a cop. People were yelling that a lady was trapped under a truck, and that she was dying. As I looked, I saw that her legs were under the tire. But then I noticed another pair of legs. I got under the truck, and there he was. Patty Brown. We both helped the woman, and she lived. But Patty Brown also helped me make it through my first day as a cop. From that day on, we were pals.

We did a lot of running, Sundays in Central Park. We solved the world's problems during those runs, but were never able to solve our own. Patty loved the city, and he used to determine the crime levels by the amount of crime-scene tape we used to see in the park. The less tape meant less crime, less dead bodies.

Patty told me a story of when he was running along the East River and a group of guys came up to him. Patty knew they were going to rob him, so he gave them one of his "stares." One of them said, "Hey, this guy is fucked up; we better get going." A few days later, Patty reads in the news that a Manhattan lawyer was killed along the East River. Patty called the police, and he became one of the star witnesses. They ended up catching the guys, and Patty was able to link them to the East River, and to the murder.

So fifteen years later, I'm a detective attending the NYPD Homicide course. It's famous—they teach all that is needed to work a homicide investigation, and cops from all over the country attend. One of the detectives who lectures at the course is this old timer, one of the most respected and decorated detectives on the job. He is teaching us about line-ups and identification of perps. He starts his lecture by telling about one of the most well-known and well-run cases he ever had. It was about a young fireman who was able to connect a gang to the scene of a homicide, and how lucky they were that this guy came forward and was able to help. I started laughing and telling my partner about Patty. At this point, the old detective was getting pissed that I was talking, so I told him that I was friends with the fireman and that he had told me the same story. The detective ended up wanting to know how Patty was, what he was doing, etc. So once again, Patty was the man, the one who came through and saved the day.

BERNIE PETTY – Detective, Waterfront Commission Police
I met Pat Brown on the streets of lower Manhattan. I had on a Seido

Karate jacket, and he stopped me and asked, "Do you train there?"

I said yes; I was a green or brown belt at the time. Pat had stopped training for a while, and said, "Oh, I wanna go back," so I encouraged him to.

So we started training together at the 12:30 class. I remember when Pat went up for his black belt, and after he got it, I said, "Pat, what was it like?" (meaning the fighting part—kumite.)

He goes, "Oh, Bernie, it was rough. Don't kid yourself, it's rough."

And we laughed. And we continued to train in the afternoons, and eventually it was my turn to go up. And I asked again, "Pat, is it really that rough?"

And he goes, "Bernie, you've got this big group and you guys are all former athletes; they're gonna come after ya." And we laughed again.

Over that period of time we had bonded—I didn't drink anymore, and neither did Pat, so we'd talk quite often and laugh about some of the gin mills. Pat was older than me; I was like a young brother to him. And he was always very kind. If he had your ear for a while, he had a very funny sense of humor, on the quiet side. Pat wasn't a loud and "out there" type of guy.

Before I became a cop, I always wanted a FDNY T-shirt, so I asked if he could get me one. He brought it by the dojo one afternoon and wouldn't take my money for it. So I started wearing the T-shirt and then started noticing that people would stop me on the street. After learning I was not a fireman, they'd go, "Who do you know at the Harlem Hilton?"

I'd say, "Pat Brown. He trains at karate with me."

"Oh my god, you know Patty Brown?"

After six or seven months of this, I say to Pat, "Do you have something you want to tell me?" And he stopped and looked at me. "What?"

I said, "I get people stopping me all over the place, asking me who do I know at the Harlem Hilton, and when I say I know you, it's like the John L. Sullivan story—people wanna 'shake the hand of the man who shook the hand of the man…'"

Of course, Pat was so modest, he just kinda mumbled an explanation.

I said, "Pat, I'll tell you what we're gonna do. You're gonna get me another T-shirt, you're gonna sign this one, and I'm gonna frame it." So we both cracked up laughing.

MICKEY CONBOY – Lieutenant, Squad Company 41, FDNY

I met Patty as a fireman in Squad 41. They had two lieutenants, Patty Brown and Jack Kleehaas. If you worked with Patty or Jack, nothin' would bother you. My first night, I remember going to a fire with Patty, and there were still plenty of fires back then. We went over to Harlem, and the Chief told us there were four people trapped on the top floor. Patty immediately told me to go back to the rig and get two more hooks. When Patty told you to do something, you did it without question. When I got back to the command post, the Chief was telling 14 Truck: "Get up to the top floor. I got Patty Brown up there. I know everything's all right, but give him a hand with the searches." And it always stuck with me—"I know everything's all right, Patty Brown's up there."

I went up and it was down to the floor, and we were taking a shellackin' and a half, and I remember coming out of there and Patty putting his arm around me and saying, "Hey, kid, how was that?" I'll always remember my first fire with him, and how happy I was to work with Patty Brown.

CHARLIE WILLIAMS – Battalion Chief, FDNY

You can be lucky when you go to a fire and find somebody, but when you do it at the rate he did it, it was more than just luck. He worked at his job; he thought, used his head, had that tunnel vision.

Medal Day **Magazine** – June 1985

Every firefighter dreads a fire in a building shaft. The fire has a clear path to the upper floors where it will mushroom out into the cockloft and compound the problems for the operating forces. The first due hose team has to take their lengths and run as fast as they can up the stairs until they get water. The race is, of course, with the vertically spreading fire.

The Ladder companies must get the roof team in position with equal rapidity because they must vent the shaft to give the fire vertical escape. This tends to negate any mushrooming tendency.

Rescue 2 responded to the fire in the six story loft building at 121 Plymouth Street on the 10-75 signal, and by the time they arrived the second alarm was being transmitted. They were ordered by the Battalion to search the buildings for occupants and for extension of fire on the upper floors.

Lieutenant Rogers split the company into teams, sending the roof-man up the aerial with the saw. Firefighter Brown and Firefighter Williams were sent to the top floor via the fire escape, while he and the third team went up the interior stairs.

Firefighter Brown and Firefighter Williams forced entry into the top floor occupancy from the fire escape and began their search. This was a commercial loft building and the occupancy they were probing occupied the entire floor. When Lieutenant Rogers reached the sixth floor, he immediately called for a line because the fire was extending out of the shaft and spreading. The two firefighters were making their search under conditions of extreme heat and smoke when the entire top floor started to light up. They were forced off the floor and back to the fire escape due to the untenable conditions. As they descended to the fifth floor on the fire escape, they heard an "urgent" message on the radio from the roof-man of Ladder 118. He and three other members were trapped on the roof, their egress being cut off by the heavy fire condition on the top floor.

Fireman Brown's instincts took over as he turned and headed back up the stairway, which was now blocked by the fire blowing out the window on the sixth floor. As a brief gust of wind drove the fire back in the window, Firefighter Brown did not hesitate as he raced past the fire and up to the roof.

When he arrived he removed his mask face-piece and yelled to the trapped members of his location and the way off the roof. The smoke and heat conditions were so severe that he could not see past his reach. The trapped members were guided to the fire escape by voice contact with Firefighter Brown. Only after all his fellow firefighters were safely off the roof and below the fire did he start down the fire escape.

As he ran past the top floor window, the fire exploded out, catching him before he could get by. He protected his face with his arms as he ran past the fire to the landing below where he collapsed. He was removed to the street by Firefighter Williams and was evacuated to the Cornell Burn Center, where he was admitted for four days with burns of the throat.

Firefighter Brown's courage, aggressiveness, and selfless devotion to duty are truly the right stuff. They are what allow the FDNY to be known as the Bravest.

CHARLIE WILLIAMS

When we went down to the floor below the fire all of a sudden he goes, gasping, "Charlie, if you have to cut me, cut me!"

And I says, "Patty, Patty, this isn't Vietnam, I don't have a Bic pen; we have doctors here." I says, "Come on, let's get downstairs."

I laugh about it; I even laughed about it then, I think, but sometimes I think, wow, he probably thought he was gonna die or choke to death, and he knew what the solution was.

MIKE McPARLAND

We had this one job on Broadhurst Avenue and 128th Street. He had just made lieutenant; I was still a fireman. It was a top floor job, and we were first due. He was comin' in second due. So my group gets up to the top and we pop the door, and the ceiling blew down and we got blown off the landing. We come barreling down the stairs, and I'm layin' on my back, on the half-landing. He's four or five steps below me, but his face is dead even with mine.

"Mike, what's up?"

I go, "Patty, it's bad up there."

He goes, "Yeah, I can see that," a little smirk on his face. A little humor in the heat of battle.

Journal Entry – September 24, 2002

My city grid is now set up strictly for function and solitude. A walk through Central Park leads me to Pat's tree, to sit on a nearby bench in the sun and simply "be." There is so much for me to assimilate. Torn out of my old life, I feel newly planted; leaning toward the sun but not sure if I am well-fertilized or properly rooting.

The dark cave of cynicism within me once easily extinguished any flicker of a flame of hope or faith. I am learning to stumble, then walk in the grey chiaroscuro of my spiritual belief system, as if Pat is shining a flashlight. Who knows, maybe he's negotiating with all the top brass in heaven, trying to get me that thermal-imaging camera to allow me to navigate in the dark.

"With courage you will dare to take risks, have the strength to be compassionate, and the wisdom to be humble. Courage is the foundation of integrity."
——Keshavan Nair

Journal Entry – March 16, 2004

The weight of an impending late-season snowstorm is pressing down. I am heading to the city for doctor appointments and art supplies, disrupting a quiet work routine at home that had already been interrupted.

The file I opened on my computer Sunday night quickly ripped out my lifeline to the outside world. It was a Trojan virus custom-designed for me—a message from my DSL service stating that I would temporarily be without e-mail, unless I opened the attachment and followed the instructions. I hesitated. It seemed a legit and official message from the friendly Verizon staff. But I certainly could live without e-mail for two days, couldn't I? And so I opened it, thus wreaking total havoc on the internal barometric pressure of my hard drive.

First, I vented to Verizon, who deflected my ire to Microsoft, where my sanguine and patient help-tech guided me through the dark paths of DOS, he in India and I in New York state. His mantra of "not to worry" ended three hours later with the jarring diagnosis that my hardware was "totally corrupted."

Of course, I had never backed up anything on my computer. It's not that I thrill to living on the edge, cybersex without condoms, but mainly because I am such a technophobe. Zip drives scared me, sitting on the shelves behind the glass counter at Staples. Even their name implied that I would never be able to grasp them. And so, I worry about My Documents. My "Pat Project." But recently I've sent my writing efforts to Gloria in Austria, along with the plan to weave the journal entries throughout the stories I collect. I needed her opinion, because she is my staunchest supporter in this endeavor. Gloria is my backup file.

We met in early February, 2002. Karma and cyberspace had once again connected the walking wounded. Gloria Pettermann never knew Pat, nor anything of firehouse culture. She read about him soon after 9/11, and a strange yet calm energy reached out to her and gently touched the pain that went so far and deep into her history.

GLORIA PETTERMANN – Author's Friend

From the beginning, Captain Patrick Brown, totally unknown to me before 9/11, has been a very precious and far-reaching inspiration. I first read about him in an Austrian newspaper. What deeply moved me was that his life was obviously very painful and difficult. But what was the real connection? Why did I feel so deeply attracted when I first learned of him? The answer is that Patrick was the first person in whom I encountered a part of myself, a hidden essence of my inner life.

Despair, depression, sadness—the leading symptoms of PTSD (post-traumatic stress disorder)—for almost twenty years, and with all my efforts, I could never fight off those emotions. I lived in a world of inner loneliness, and with an often distorted and painful state of mind that can come over one like a shockwave. And yet I had many friends, a good career—outwardly seeming quite normal and reasonable, strong, funny, and outgoing. But behind that curtain of efficiency, anxiety and depression prevented relationships from becoming really close and warm and meaningful.

I have always been a spiritual seeker, and have struggled a lot on this road because of my very dark and ambivalent concept of God. Too many terrible events in the history of mankind, too much pain and suffering of innocents all over the world, too much horror in my own childhood. Growing older, I was aware that there were also many good and reliable people around, but this knowledge was very abstract and theoretical, and somehow never really touched me.

Reading about Patrick Brown let me understand that people can be very good and very problematic at the same time. By dealing in such an honest and brave way with the trials in his life, Patrick became a shining example for me. I was fascinated by how he was able to transform a life marked by tragic events and terrible losses into such commitment to others; I admired his progress into the realm of heroic altruism and valor.

At the beginning of February 2002, I went to New York for a sort of "inner pilgrimage" to honor not only Patrick but also all the other rescue workers who had sacrificed their lives to save others. I had received a totally unexpected contact to close friends of Patrick's, who shared many inspiring stories about him, and who guided me to places he loved: the Ladder 3 firehouse, Yoga Center Jivamukti, St. Francis Xavier church, and the East Village. I had to walk for hours in Central Park to absorb and process my impressions. And there I also saw Pat's tree, planted in his honor.

When I learned that Patrick's remains were found, I was profoundly saddened. Until then, I had focused on his courage, his deep respect and concern for his colleagues, his way into the Light. Now, I could sense in my heart the brutal reality of his death—his last moments among the severely injured people he refused to abandon in that shaking and burning building, the horrible pancaking noise of the collapse, and the end of it all. I felt more than ever the impact of the loss of Patrick and the other gallant rescuers. At the same moment, a new understanding caused me to appreciate in a much deeper way the total solidarity between rescuers and victims. That, because of the ultimate sacrifice of people like Patrick, those victims had a caring human presence close to them, abiding with them.

My partly very dark concept of God has greatly changed, and so did my concept of the essence of human beings. I am convinced that Death is not the final point of existence, and that persons who lived their lives for others are continuing in many ways to help those who are still on this earth.

Patrick Brown has forever touched my soul. He was and is for me a kind of "catalyst," a mentor and messenger delivering hope and patience, as well as a new and radiant vision of the human condition where love and hope will have the very last word.

BARBARA MARCUS – Creator of "The Face of Courage" Project
After the tragic events of September 11, 2001, many of us searched our hearts to find a way to help alleviate the unbearable grief and contribute to the healing process. My thoughts as an artist kept returning to a simple concept: to provide families of the missing uniformed rescue workers with portraits of their loved ones. I also envisioned the portraits traveling in a nation-wide exhibition before being donated to the families who have suffered so much. This intuitive reaction was the beginning of an incredible journey.

Starting with the envelopes—manila envelopes arrived every day, containing photographs of the men who sacrificed their lives attempting to save the lives of others. Along with the photographs sent by family members were profoundly moving letters describing their loved ones. This information was to be given to the artists responsible for painting the portraits—a solemn responsibility taken very seriously by us all. My friends and family would tell you that I was pretty much an emotional wreck during those months. I felt tremendous pressure to try to visually resurrect the men that I had never met—to do the very best I could for their families. As the organizer of this project, I was under a great deal of stress, having made a commitment that came from the heart, but had no administrative, financial, or strategic support.

I knew nothing about Captain Patrick Brown prior to receiving his envelope. When I came face to face with the handsome man in dress uniform, I did a little investigating and was overwhelmed with his astonishing accomplishments and the outpouring of tributes by so many people from all walks of life.

My studio is the converted loft of a barn in the Maryland countryside. During those months, it served not only as a workplace for the nine portraits that I was to paint, but also as storage for portraits of the heroes done by artists all over the country. Every morning, entering that space was like walking into a church—all of those faces watching me. It was humbling and it was overwhelming. But one can't paint and cry at the same time. Even under such emotional circumstances, painting is also an analytical process that must be approached with objectivity. When starting to paint on a white canvas, first it is important to do a very solid drawing. The layers of paint that follow build the surface, and while analyzing all of the subtle relationships that build a human face, the individual begins to emerge. As Paddy's portrait developed, I felt myself more and more in his presence. He seemed to be observing me painting him. I felt a quiet sense of encouragement. I sometimes felt a teasing sort of humor. And during my really dark moments in that studio, I felt overwhelming compassion emanating from that canvas—from someone who understood. I am sure that all of those traits exist in the photograph. But they certainly became stronger for me in the painting process. I also have to admit, as a woman, I had a very strong intuition that this man's masculinity is undeniable.

When the painting was finished, I hung it on the wall with the other portraits. As I continued working on other paintings of wonderful firefighters and police officers, I always felt Paddy's quiet support and approval. I have no doubt that he was a great leader not only for his men, but also for people in many areas of his life. His leadership stemmed not from ego, but from character. As for The Face of Courage project, I am delighted to be able to say that fifty-eight portraits have traveled to twelve venues around the country. These venues include state and federal buildings, college and commercial galleries, and museums. Tens of thousands of people have been profoundly moved by and will never forget the exhibit. Our exhibition sign-in book is full of gratitude for the heroes and for the cathartic effect experienced through this project. Wonderful volunteers have made this monumental endeavor a reality.

As for me, I will never be the same, and I will never forget Paddy Brown. I have a photograph of his portrait on my office wall. When things get tough, I subconsciously glance at Captain Patrick Brown, and he always nudges me to make the right decision— with a wink.

"The tragedy of war is that it uses man's best to do man's worst"

——Harry Emerson Fosdick

Journal Entry – March 23, 2004

In the course of the last week, world events have taken a turn for the worse, resulting in a cold, dull knot of dread snowballing through my nervous system. This feeling of futility can stain the simple doings of everyday life and spread into future plans, like bad red wine on a linen tablecloth. Of course, my routine had already been interrupted, and with the computer down, I was still on shaky ground.

I remember when I was a child lying in bed at night with my teddy bear, the Visitor would sneak up and blanket my thoughts with fear before I drifted off to sleep. Death. My young intellect regarded Death as The End. Nothing, no more Me or anything I loved doing, forever and ever, Amen. Even at that early age, I wasn't buying into the notion of frolicking in heaven with my pets, or being held again in my father's arms. I was a ten-year-old pessimist/agnostic/realist. The thought of Death would visit me often, and keep me awake.

The Visitor has changed. Now what keeps me awake at night is the idea of living in our deteriorating world. A world torn with terror and destruction, allowing the worst of human nature to spread like the viruses that invade our bodies and our computers.

Before the Internet started bringing video-taped beheadings into our homes, the toe-hold for this visual assault was taking place in our living rooms in 1967. The war in Vietnam was served up daily on the evening news, as we sat in front of our television sets with our Swanson TV dinners. All across America, and in Queens Village, too.

Like all young men (boys, really) on a battlefield, Pat had experienced death and horror up close and far more personally than I can ever imagine. He left home at seventeen and joined the Marines. In 1972, he was in Vietnam, at the point when we were quagmired chin-deep in an unwinnable war. He must have known it even before he shipped out. I was privy to a little of what propelled him out into that preferable hell a half a globe away.

We had talked of visiting Vietnam together, after marrying. Vietnam was newly open to tourism, and we pored over the map, planning our trip. Pat was looking through the lens of twenty years, trying to imagine a place that didn't evoke night terrors, mud, and death. My own lens was rosy and naïve, focused on the romantic notion of adventure with my new fiancé. We would shop the markets and buy conical hats, and luxuriate in refurbished French-colonial hotels with rattan overhead fans. We would visit the DMZ, and I would protect him from the landmines of traumatic memory.

And we had talked of adopting a Vietnamese baby. Healthy, fertile, and fit, we could have had our own. But Pat had wanted to adopt, from guilt, no doubt, yet another burden that a boy fighting in a war shouldn't have to bear.

Pat had a burning need to share some of that guilt, and he prepared me by telling me he had three stories; did I want to hear them? And so I braced myself for his Vietnam trilogy, fearing details of Mai Lai proportions. Instead I heard of three incidents that, yes, were horrific. But they were well within the "normal range" of atrocity that we seem to accept in wartime. Still, these were boys. And to a nice Catholic boy, whose mother once denied that the blood oozing from a roast in the oven was indeed blood, the carnage of war was all too real. And so the boy became a warrior, eventually returning to a life fighting fire as aggressively as any battle in Vietnam. Being so close to Death sanctified Life. Pat was never a "death wish" junkie. But he was wired to push himself to the absolute max. Saving lives became his own salve, his own salvation.

PAT BROWN – *Time Magazine* – Sept. 6, 1999

I was in the Marines in Vietnam, and fire fighting is like war. If a life is in there, you go in, you get 'em out—even when it's black and smoky, your body's burning up and you're fighting the natural urge to run. The F.D.N.Y. trains you to be aggressive and hyper vigilant, not to take stupid risks. We don't do this for sport or for thrills or money. You're risking your life to save somebody. That's what makes this job special. We take risks for a greater good.

Journal Entry – March 23, 2004, *continued*

A few days after my first date with Pat, I got a call from him. His close friend Pete McLaughlin, a younger and sunnier version of Pat in Queens Rescue 4, had just tragically died in a fire. Pat delivered the news in a matter-of-fact way that befitted his experience as captain in the fire department. He wanted me to tell Kaicho, the head of our karate school, that he would be missing classes that week in early October, and asked if I would pass along the reason why (fully documented in an article in the *Daily News*, Pat pictured with the grieving family.) I said, "Of course," and was numbed. I took the article to my therapy appointment and told Barbara of my quandary—that I had just started dating a nice guy but that I didn't think I was equipped to be a comfort to him. In just one meeting over dinner, I sensed that he was a very deep and serious man who had experienced much loss and pain. And now this. I had never even been to a funeral. I was no "Earth Mother." I felt so inadequate, uncomfortable, and yet couldn't just pull out. Her wise advice to me was to simply be myself, be open, be there. And so when he called me again at the end of the week to go out to dinner, I wanted to see him. But not in a public setting, after such personal loss. I invited him to my apartment in Brooklyn for whatever I was already cooking. Pat showed up at the door, met my cats, shared my dinner, and sat on the sofa with me. And we talked. And talked. And the words flowed, the tears flowed, and I found that I wanted nothing more but to comfort him, and try to understand how to transcend grief.

SEANE CORN – Yoga Instructor

I used to work at Peggy Sue's, on University Place and 10th Street, back in the early 90s. I was probably around twenty years old. Terry Quinn owned the club, and it drew in a lot of firemen, a lot of people. I did the door, and sometimes I did the bar. One night Pat and I started talking; he had come off duty at 2:00 or 3:00 a.m., and we closed around four. I got up to leave and was gonna walk home like I always did, down to Avenue B and 12th Street. And Pat was outraged. Absolutely outraged that I was going to walk home that late. He couldn't believe that I did it every night.

I didn't know him well; at that point I had only met him a few times. He was living in Stuyvesant Town, and that was across from Avenue B. During that first walk, I found out about his history—being an alcoholic, and joining AA, and the recovery that he had done. And about Vietnam. A lot of his life story came up. He was really philosophical, and we just talked. And he walked me home. No ulterior motive, no asking me out on a date, nothing. It was just, "All right, see ya."

Next time I'm at work, 3:00 a.m., Pat shows up after his shift. "Are you ready to go? C'mon." Walks me home. Same thing—we talk about life, and I learn more about his journey. I was really struck by just how soulful this man was. I had no idea what kind of fireman he was; I did not know to what kind of level of hero... I just thought he was one of Terry's friends, like someone I grew up with, basically. I grew up in New Jersey and I know this "type." They're good guys. I didn't know then *how* good Pat was, but I definitely had a sense of his depth.

The next time I'm at work, same thing, but this time he shows up at a quarter to four, right before closing. He comes over and I ask him, "Why are you here so late? What time did you get off your shift?" He hadn't worked that night. He deliberately woke up in the middle of the night, came to the club, and walked me home.

This went on for about a year. Sometimes we'd sit on the stoop along 14th Street and talk. Occasionally we talked about drugs and alcohol, which I was doing at that time, but not hardcore. He really made me question, and talked to me like a person. And it was clear he cared about me. I sometimes wondered, What are his intentions? Not once did he cross that line. There was no assumption, nothing. It was really just out of kindness.

During this time I started to find out a little bit about what he did. Little stories emerged, but not from Pat—from the guys. They were like, "Do you have any idea?" He made this rescue, that rescue… Then, there was a really big rescue in Times Square—it was all over the news—and that's when I started to realize how incredible a person Pat was.

That year of knowing Pat was a flash in time, but it was a significant experience. I was so young, and had never been treated with that much respect and concern since I had moved to New York City. Now, looking back, I feel really privileged, because even though I really didn't "get" who Pat was, he was definitely a hero to me. He did a spectacular act of kindness, every night.

PAULA SUPERTI — Pat's NYU Classmate

I was in a writing class with Pat at NYU in 1990. We became friends through sharing our personal essays and feeling a bit out of place among the younger students. I was married and seven months pregnant, and my best friend was dying of AIDS. We could not have had more divergent times or places in our lives, from the outside, but that was the thing about a truly enlightened human being like Pat. He was deeply kind in the most humble way possible. Before I knew it, he was popping by my place for dinner once in a while, and later, in retrospect, I realized he was just checking up on me, just to make sure all was well, or if I needed a friend—a friend like Pat, the best there could ever be. It is hard to imagine that with his way of being, just how many people he affected, and how badly his spirit is missed.

And this is the hardest thing about long-term grief—what we all do with it. This is the damn hard thing. Pat was a hero in every sense of the word, but the meaning of that word doesn't convey the depth of our collective loss. What category do we have for Pat when baseball players are the heroes of our day? We need more Pat Browns, who will model that role for us. I never stop thinking about him when I think of the best sort of man a man can be. His qualities of humility, courage, authenticity, empathy, and strength are the essential foundation that I wish for in my own son. When I see them there, I think of Pat. He has, in his death, become symbolic. That is the fundamental nature of a hero.

And this is the thing: He was just being Pat Brown; he wasn't trying, like some sort of method actor, to be a deeply good, sincere, and caring person. He was truly the kind of human being that we can all aspire to be, which is simply this: genuine in our striving to be kind, helpful, and courageous. Not because there is some accolade waiting at the other end of our gestures, but because there is only us, no one else, and then death. Even in his death, he was serving, and there could be no bigger crime than forgetting all of the Pat Browns who served us on that inexcusable day.

And so I beg everyone to consider this: With all of the rehashing of September 11th, all of the media regurgitating endlessly every factoid about what happened—which simply numbs us all to the harsh reality of the catastrophe—dare to exempt yourself from the uselessness of all of that white noise and meditate on how, today, we could all be a friend to someone, a friend like Pat Brown, because that is the only way I can see that the future holds any promise.

MARTHA HARTLEY — Pat's and Author's Friend
I had just moved to Manhattan's East Village from San Francisco. It was 1986; I was one and a half years clean and sober, and I knew absolutely no

one in the city. I immediately set out to begin my new life with three things—attend AA/NA meetings, sign myself up for karate classes, and enroll in school.

Soon after I first entered the St. Mark's Place AA basement room, I noticed through the street windows a fire truck pull up. I thought, in that dark, run-down building, a fire would be the end of us all. Alone in NY, that's not how I wanted to go. Much to my relief, there were no sirens, just a man in uniform slipping in for a few moments. Now, I've seen firemen driving their trucks to grocery stores for years, every city, every neighborhood I've lived in, but I'd never seen this. It crossed my mind that this guy must be having a really bad day. Something terrible has happened "out there" and he needs the power of the program at this particular time. Most of us do, at some time or another. But it wasn't just once. It happened quite frequently and I was becoming impressed. I'd use any excuse not to go to meetings, and here was Pat Brown, going out of his way to get what little he could during a routine day at one of the most stressful jobs there is.

After a while, I noticed this same man in my karate classes. Although it was not uncommon to share the program and our dojo, we recognized each other with complete respect. Pat and I always bowed to each other and exchanged smiles and simple greetings. He was consistently warm, humble, sincere and devoted. It was evident, written within his demeanor, every day. Yet again, I was most impressed.

Soon before 9/11 happened, I had relapsed and was in rehab. We were not allowed to watch television, read the newspapers, or make phone calls. My mother reluctantly told me what had occurred. She knew I had left many loved ones behind when I left New York City. I was horribly concerned for everyone I could think of but never did I imagine the world would lose all those that were so brave and important to our communities. When I left rehab, I began to make contact and piece together the puzzle. Many of my friends had left the city; one of them died. That was Pat. Months went by and I heard that they had found Pat.

I was so unbelievably relieved that his family and loved ones could put him to rest. We all share his incredible strength and spirit in everything he did. We miss him.

Only in the words of Patti Smith can I express: "Paths that cross will cross again." See ya Pat.

BARBARA KANESHIGE — Author's Friend

My entire relationship with Pat was little more than dinner and a movie, and yet the profound effect he had on my life allows me to count myself among the many whom he saved, enriched, or changed forever. Patrick Brown was my hero. Then again, as one of the most decorated firefighters in the city of New York, Pat was pretty much everyone's hero.

He was neither tall nor large, as height and weight are measured, and so I am reassured to know that our lives are measured by our reach and not our grasp. Pat changed my life by expanding my world. He showed me that the door to heroism is larger than heroic acts. Through Pat I learned that the foundation of heroism is love.

Pat loved me. I could tell from the minute Sharon introduced us. He looked at me and shook my hand, and all the fears that an unworthy fiancé would distance me from a good friend vanished. I knew that Sharon had found someone who loved her, someone special who would love me, too, because I was her friend.

After dinner we took the subway, and Pat dragged me to the wall of the station. He always insisted that anyone he knew wait for the train by the wall. He had wrapped up too many bodies of people who had been pushed onto the tracks. I have been standing against the wall ever since. I have also dragged everyone I have ever traveled by train with to the wall.

I know the odds are slim that this saved my life, or any of my friends, from a psycho subway-pusher. Still, the story and the sentiment Pat shared is like the Master Card ad—priceless. It told me that Pat cared. And in passing on Pat's message that someone cares that we are safe, the world becomes a better place.

Learning of Pat's death, I knew I had an obligation to help carry the banner that was dropped when he fell. It was too heavy to pick up alone. I asked for help.

On October 11, 2001, one month after 9/11, my calls were answered. I initiated a yard-sale fund-drive from my home in Maui, and that Saturday afternoon, $7000 was raised in the names of Patrick Brown and his good friend Captain Terry Hatton, whom I had met on his honeymoon. My firm belief that Patrick Brown's life far exceeded his grasp was confirmed.

That movie and dinner we went to eight years ago when I was visiting New York? I don't remember where we ate, or what the film was. But years later I remember Pat loved me, not because of who I was, but rather who *he* was—always the hero.

I love you, Pat.

Journal Entry – April 1, 2004

I changed seats twice, in an effort to get away from the chatty exuberance of four college-age girls. My head feels like it could crack, and things will only get worse as day turns to night. I am in pre-colonoscopy mode— only drinking water and apple juice until midnight, then nothing but the phosphosoda until the procedure tomorrow morning.

It all comes with turning fifty—more tests, more procedures, navigating menopause. For the most part, I am okay with this aging business. Maybe I'm lucky. I feel my life has balance; my passions involve me and hopefully "evolve" me. I have many friends made from earliest childhood through the past year. I was once like these four from Poughkeepsie who chatter on about boys, clothes, cell phones, makeup, cars, sports, school—I notice how ungenerous I've become in some ways since 9/11.

The innocent narcissism of "American Youth" seems an inalienable right that we as a culture have bred and nurtured. I just wish the sense of entitlement didn't so often accompany it. We presume too many other world cultures would be better off if they embraced the American Way. Somehow it seems to factor in as a byproduct of what is fueling the exuberance of the four girls who are giving me a headache.

If I were nineteen, maybe by now I would be exactly like them. I might have put 9/11 behind me. But I am fifty, and it is in me, and no amount of medical scraping is going to change that.

Journal Entry – April 5, 2004
I emerged from Beth Israel Hospital feeling as light as a butterfly, my cocoon of apprehension shed along with the hospital gown and the disposable sponge-y slippers, each embossed with a smiley face on the toes. The second procedure did not result in a perforated uterus, a hysterectomy, or even mild cramps.

I had half expected some right-winged "morality payback" for the decade plus of worry-free sex; in the incubation period of the AIDS epidemic, it tended to be spontaneous and serendipitous. Then, after meeting Pat, monogamous and often. With Pat and me, water was seeking and finding its own level, and for nine months, we were bonded in the life raft, with hope and determination as well as love, kismet, and, yes, sex.

Sitting on Pat's small eating table was a homemade mug, a slightly crude joke gift from the guys at Rescue 2 (all with Ph.D.s in the subject of Black Humor), with an AIDS reference painted on that I had asked him about. Apparently Pat was a tad more risk-taking as a rescuer than some of them in the early era of the full-blown AIDS epidemic. He would apply mouth-to-mouth with not a moment's hesitation to anyone who needed it, often on the drug-infested streets where shared needles were a way of life that pushed the H.I.V. rate to record numbers. He never considered his own safety, never stopped to pass judgment on a person who might be fueling the devastation of lives by selling crack cocaine, heroin, or any of the dozens of pills and potions that kept Bed-Stuy, Brownsville, Crown Heights, Harlem, and so many other neighborhoods stuck in the cycle of drugs and poverty through out the 70s, 80s, and early 90s. And if he could help save a victim not only of fire but of drug abuse, he would do it in a heartbeat with his breath of life.

MICKEY CONBOY

There was a fire on Walton Avenue one night in the South Bronx. I was driving in Rescue 3 and pulled into the block, and the covering captain Phil Ruvulo was screaming, "There's people trapped on the top floor! Rescue to the top floor!"

There was a man, a civilian, slamming his head off the hood of a car, screaming, "My babies are trapped!"

I grabbed him and asked, "Where are your kids trapped?" And he said, "The top floor!"

I remember lookin' at this old Civil War building, twenty feet by forty feet, heavy fire still blowin' out of the second floor, and sayin', "Those kids are up there." As I ran past the second floor I was fortunate enough to have that "sixth sense" that I learned from Patty Brown, to know where people were. Patty always said, "Position, position, position." I used to pick his brain—How do you do this? How do you do that?

And everything always was, "Oh, it's simple, Mick; it's 'position, position, position.'" Yeah, I thought, it's simple for *you*! Everybody else is tryin' to figure out what the fuck you're doin'!

I remember goin' up, getting' into that floor, and thinking God'll put me in the right spot. I reached into that bathroom, over the marble threshold, and I felt the kid's leg. And I reached in and pulled that leg with everything I had, and the leg's not movin'. And I said, "Something's wrong." I reached in farther and crawled into that bathroom, and I realized her legs, her arms, were entangled in her sister's, so I untangled them and I pulled them both. A lieutenant came around the corner to help, and I passed those two kids out. I remembered Patty saying, "Position, position, position." I went back to that bathroom, reached into the bath tub, and found the mother. As I reached in under her arms to pull her out of the tub, I felt something that wasn't right. I reached under her left arm, and I felt her five-year-old son. To my disbelief, there were three kids and a mother in that room.

Pete McLaughlin, a good friend of Patty's, was there at that time, and said, "Mick, where are ya? Where's the people?"

And I says, "Pete, thank god you're here." I grabbed her and pulled her with everything I had to give her to Pete, and Pete took that lady down to the street. So I grabbed that five-year-old and ran down two flights of stairs to the street, and I'll never forget seeing Patty Brown standing there. I said, "Patty, you got a resuscitator?"

And he goes, "Yeah."

And I say, "All right, let's go!" As I start to run with the kid, I look down… Patty's idea of a resuscitator was his doing mouth-to-mouth. As he had done so many times before, and did so many times after. And I'll never forget, as I ran up Walton Avenue, how he never missed a step, and I'm tellin' you, I was running as fast as I could with that five-year-old in my arms.

The mother and two girls succumbed to their injuries. Young Steven Brown lived because of Patty Brown's "resuscitator."

"The ultimate measure of a man is not where he stands in moments of comfort and convenience, but where he stands at times of challenge and controversy." ——Martin Luther King, Jr.

Journal Entry – June 14, 2005

I submerge myself early into a premature dog day of summer, like a teabag set to steep in the city's humidity. The reason for coming in is a street dedication to Captain Terry Hatton of Rescue 1, by invitation from his mother, who sells me vitamins and is full of sweetness and positive messages. Pat and Terry, Terry and Pat—two friends, two different sides of the same coin of extreme dedication and application of selflessness in both saving lives and improving the FDNY. Two different styles, with Pat having seniority in both experience and age. Terry was rewarded with the captaincy of Rescue 1 that Pat had wanted passionately (and according to many, deserved. There still are those on the job who feel that protocol and the right thing was for Terry to step aside.) But Terry swayed the doubters with his leadership and his motto of "outstanding or unacceptable," and any professional rift between them was quelled by the depth of their friendship, and the karma of Pat's finding his place in the tough and elite Ladder 3.

I arrive sweating to West 43rd Street and edge into the cool shadows inside the firehouse. On a wall full of history and photos, I zero in on a group shot taken after the 1991 roof rope rescue in Times Square. The shock of Pat's young profile—the intensity of the brow, the strong jaw line, the hair flopping over his famous "Eddie Munster" widow's peak— catches me off guard. Sometimes I forget he was so handsome.

Back on the steaming street, I do a double-take: I spot a similar profile, with the same piercing blue eyes but a softer jaw. It is his sister Carolyn. Being eleven years his junior would make her about the same age as Pat in that photo. Carolyn is instantly recognized as she mingles with the retired firefighters who knew her brother when she was just a little girl; the resemblance is that strong. She hears the stories and fills in the gaps, and clearly enjoys the comradeship that is bestowed on her by virtue of blood. Her pride in Pat is palpable.

PAT BROWN – *The New York Times Magazine* – June, 2001 (interview with Tom Downey, also included in the prologue of Downey's book, *The Last Men Out*)

You could tell by the guy's voice that something was going on. We were ordered to respond to Seventh Avenue and Forty-eighth Street. They're starting to say on the radio that there's a bad fire— people are trapped. So we get there, and two people are hanging out different windows. We started charging up the stairs. It was a twelve-story building. I was so pumped I don't even remember that being a hindrance. I've been on the job a long time, and I've been around real tragedy—situations where our guys were killed. Even if you don't do anything wrong, you can get killed on this job. I'm always trying to be ready for whatever can happen.

I ran up to the roof because I wanted to see where these guys were trapped. There was nobody up there, but they were construct- ing a building right across the street and these construction workers were screaming and pointing below me. I had to climb up on the parapet to see where this guy was. There he was, right under me, hanging from the window ledge, ready to jump. The fire was roar- ing right next to him, so I ran back to the stairwell and I told the others to get up there.

"Hold on," I screamed to the victim. He looked up at me as if he was braced to jump. "We're coming to get you," I said. He wasn't responsive. He just looked.

Pat Barr was carrying the lifesaving rope. It's always been a tradition everywhere I know that if you're carrying the rope, you're the guy they're going to lower. For safety, we take a separate rope, and we tie it to the guy who's lowering the rescuer. He's attached to an object on the roof so he doesn't go over.

Now we realize we don't have anywhere substantial to tie this rope the way we're supposed to. This guy was going to jump any minute, any minute. Even thinking of it, I get all upset. As a lieutenant, I could have said that we aren't doing this. And the guy would have died. I could have said that it's too dangerous, and nobody would have said a word. If I had finagled around and said, "Break the wall so we can tie off and have a safety line," he would have been gone. The victim was four or five feet below, looking up at me. It was either let's do it or not.

I just said, "I know we can do it. Here's what we can do: Kevin, brace yourself against the wall. We're going to hold you down." So we tied Pat Barr to Kevin Shea, and Pat went over on the rope. Now Pat's hanging thirteen flights above the street, attached only to Kevin, and we're slowly lowering him. I was scared to death. In 1980, a guy from my firehouse was killed from the same thing. He had rescued another firefighter, and the rope snapped and they fell to their death. That guy, Larry Fitzpatrick, was a good friend of mine. I had been a fireman three or four years when he got killed. Now here I was directing the same thing.

This victim was on the precipice of life. It was seconds. Pat Barr grabbed him, and that dead weight stretched the rope so intensely that Kevin, who was lowering Pat from the roof, started pinioning right up. At this point, Paddy O'Keefe jumped on top of Kevin to hold him down, anchoring him to the roof. We lowered Barr and the victim to the floor below, and they're just hanging there outside the window. I'm screaming on the radio for somebody. The fire is roaring ten feet from them. None of our guys on that floor below the fire knew they were there. If the fire had come out, it would have burned the rope.

Pat swung around and broke the windowpane with his hand, while still holding on to the victim. A fireman saw them, and the guys all ran over and pulled them in. The construction workers started cheering. Everybody's going "All right!" But I remember saying to Paddy (O'Keefe), "There's another guy trapped on the other side."

As we came to where the guy was trapped, another fireman from Ladder 24, this guy Ray McCormack, came up to the roof. All I said was, "You got a belt to lower him?" He said yeah. I told him, "Okay, you're going to lower Kevin." And we did exactly the same thing as the first one. We saved both these guys. I was elated. But there was no rah-rah to it. I was humbled.

I had nightmares for weeks about what could have happened. There are so many unknowns in this job. Sometimes I wonder. It worked out great; it worked out fine. But even now I think: Man, oh man, that was such a close call. It was the right thing to do, but it was right on the edge.

MICKEY CONBOY

A couple of years after my first fire with Patty, Patty moved on and was covering Rescue 1, and there was a fire in Times Square. I was assigned to Rescue 3 at the time, as the second rescue going down to Midtown, so you know it's going bad.

They gave the progress report: "We've done one roof rope rescue and are in the process of doing another." And I just remember saying, "Oh shit, this is going bad." We got there, the Chief says, "We got members burnt; I want you to move that line!" When we got up there on the top floor, it was total chaos, and I remember hearing on the radio the calm voice of Patty Brown: "We got the second one."

I remember afterward saying to another firefighter, Sean, "How the hell did they do this roof rope rescue?" And a truck company standing there saying, "That's a bunch of bullshit—nobody tied off here and went off the roof." And I just looked over and said, "They don't know Patty Brown." And Sean looked at me. "Yup. He did it." And he jumped up on the parapet and looked down. "Yup. He did it." And I remember saying, "They don't know who they were dealing with. Patty could make this happen. If somebody could make guys believe in themselves, to dangle off a roof of a building, it was Patty Brown."

PAT BARR – FDNY, Retired

When they were tying me up to go over the parapet, I was talking to Pat about what we gotta do. They still hadn't found a substantial object to tie the rope to. So this was kind of new, as far as guys holdin' me with the rope. So I was very concerned, obviously, and I dismounted partially, still holding on by my arms and my hands. And he climbed up right next to me, face to face, and the last thing I said to him was "Don't drop me, please!" and I remember he looked me in the eyes and says, "Patty, I got you; don't worry about it." That helped. It still wasn't guaranteed or anything, but it made it easier, going over that edge. When I was on the rope with José, we were still danglin', and I knew Pat was up there. I couldn't think of a better guy to have up there.

ROOF ROPE TV NEWS COVERAGE – 1991 (interview excerpt)

Interviewer: You're real proud of your guys.
Pat: These guys? Fifteen years on the job, most courageous act I ever saw. These guys hangin' thirteen floors. Right Patty? Kevin? (Embraces both.)

JOSÉ GALLEGOS – Musician Rescued From Roof

I think about Pat all the time. To me, he's still alive. He's very deep inside. I carry him in a very special place in my heart.

Because of his efforts and his tremendous passion for his job, he saved my life. I really thought I was going to die. The minute I saw a pair of boots hanging over the parapet above and a very loud voice shouting at me, I don't know, it was like a voice from the sky giving me courage. He directed, orchestrated *every*thing—this group of guys, Rescue 1. It was May 14, 1991. Patty Barr came down on the rope and grabbed me. When I got downstairs to the first floor, I was very confused. Once I got the bear hug from Patty Barr, I passed out. After that, it was a very nice period of my life where I shared moments with all the guys at Rescue 1. I went to their firehouse—they really gave me a warm welcome; they even cooked for me! I felt so very happy. There was a moment where we forgot all about the fire; we were just sharing things and talking about life—talking about books and music and baseball. Pat Brown and I became very good friends. We "connected." It was a very beautiful friendship, and I learned to love him like my own brother. I miss him dearly, but my sadness turns to happiness every time I think of him, when I remember how he was and how we shared very good moments. God makes things happen. He put Pat into my life for a reason, and I feel inspired by him, by his spirit, by his sense of humor, by his appreciation for music, by his passion. By how he connected with all of us. He lifts my spirit and gives me courage to continue living and working and moving forward.

Pat, I know that everything you did in life was with a purpose. You certainly did what you had to do. You lived your mission. I love you, Pat. You are always with me. I am always with you.

GEORGE MERRILL – Wilmington Delaware Fire Department

I first learned about Pat by seeing a TV clip of the daring rope rescue that Pat and the other members of Rescue 1 had made from a roof top without using a fixed anchor point. I was in the fire service at the time and was impressed by this operation. A *Firehouse* magazine was always lying around the fire station, I enjoyed reading the heroism awards and learning about the different types of saves performed by firefighters around the country.

When 9/11 occurred, I was sickened by the loss of the 343 brother firefighters at the World Trade Center, and when I heard that Pat was among them, I was not surprised, but saddened. I went to Pat's funeral mass at the Cathedral of Saint Patrick on November 9, 2001 and was astonished by the amount of people who attended. This was the first time that I had been to New York and felt that the FDNY members would not really want to talk to a firefighter from a small town, since there was so many of us in their city, and the circumstances of that time with all the missing people and funeral services every day. I was mistaken. They were very appreciative to have us visit and be there for the services. I spoke to many that day and found out much more about Paddy Brown. I learned that Pat was Irish as I am, and that he was a fellow Marine. One thing they all said was that as famous as Pat had become, he did not have an ego; he had time to talk to everyone who spoke to him.

Many of my brother firefighters and Marines really don't have the words to describe how we feel about Pat's life and all he gave to us. People in today's society admire athletes and have them as role models and heroes. When you learn about the legacy of Pat Brown, there is no comparison; in my mind he is the true American hero.

TOM KELLY

Patty was well-known on the job as a very aggressive fireman, and I was always impressed that he had the presence of mind there to remember his role: that he was to run the operation and not be the guy to go over. So many guys who become legends as firemen make terrible bosses. I was always impressed how he ran that job.

MIKE SHEPHERD

I met Patty in Gleason's Gym, when they moved to Brooklyn. I was an eighteen-year-old kid, and he came in, and I saw the Rescue 2 shirt and I said, "Are you a fireman?" And he said, "Yeah."

I said, "Well, my grandfather and great-grandfathers were firemen, and my grandmother was a matron." And we just kinda hit it off.

I called him right after the roof rope rescue and I said, "Patty, I don't know if you remember me—I was a young kid in Gleason's Gym when I met you."

"Yeah! Yeah, I remember you!"

And I said, "That was a great rescue that you guys made today. I just want you to know that I think you're one of the bravest firemen that I know, and I'm happy that I met you."

I know there's a lot of guys who were jealous of him, because I know a lot of firemen in my neighborhood and I always mentioned his name, and they're kinda like, "Yeah…I know him, I know him…"

And I'd say, "He's one of the best firemen that you'd ever want to meet!" But they didn't know him as a person. They just knew he wore a Rescue 2 helmet, and they hated Rescue 2 because Rescue 2 caught all their mistakes.

I was an iron worker, restorin' Carnegie Hall, so he'd come down in the rig. My friend looks at Patty and says, "Jeez! You'd think you were ten feet tall, the way he was talkin' about you!"

Look, I'm a Brooklyn guy, and I pretty much say what's on my mind. He loved that. He'd call me up and say, "That was great! What you said…" We were both birds of the same feather, you know. He lost his mother when he was a young guy; we had brothers and sisters. We all had problems. We went to boxing. He went into the military. We wanted to be firemen our whole lives. We both were in the Actor's Guild—I did commercials, magazines; he did soaps. We were always in the public eye, like, a lot of people knew us. Patty was a little more humble than me.

He had more medals than he knew what to do with. I remember goin' to his house, and he had them all in a Chinese soup jar. You're only allowed to wear a certain amount. Three down and three across. But he had the old soup container full of medals that he didn't wear. Then he told me he won the Silver Star in Vietnam. I think actually he did show it to me with the flag and star. But what I hear is nobody can find it, or whatever. I said to him, if he had a child, they could go to West Point for free.

I'd always ask him, "Why didn't you ever get married and have children?"

And he said, "Because I love the job too much. I just don't have the time."

Definitely, I looked up to him as a mentor. I said, "Patty, I want to work with *you*." He said, "You gotta go to a Rescue company; I'm gonna get you into a Rescue. Otherwise you'll waste your talents." I'm in S.O.C. now—Squad 41. Patty worked there.

You know, he wanted Rescue 1, big time. But he couldn't bump the weight that Hatton had. And he also said on TV, "Let me talk to the Mayor." It just didn't go over well. Patty always had respect for Terry. He said, "Mike, Terry's a good fireman." The guys in Rescue 1 wanted Pat to be their boss in the worst way, but knew it was all political.

Patty came out to my graduation from probie school; his arm was in a sling from rotator-cuff surgery. He drove his car out there... Says a lot about the guy, ya know?

Me and him are walkin' thru StuyTown—we see smoke comin' from a scaffold, a one-story wood scaffold coverin' the sidewalk. He goes, "There's a fire up there; somethin's burnin'." And I hop on the fire escape, climb through the barbed wire, and I see that somebody flicked a cigarette out, and the timbers were burnin'. He says, "I'm gonna call it in," and I started laughin'. You know, I could piss on it and put it out. And he calls it in, and he says, "We'll give them the run; they need the runs." So I think 24 Truck comes down, and the can man is s'posed to get up there and put it out. Says to me, "How did you get up there?" And Patty says, "Well, *you* figure it out, how to get up there!" To me: "What's this kid askin' you? He's gotta find his *own* way."

I told him I was goin' on vacation (early September 2001), and he called me and left a message on my machine. I wish I would've saved it.

"Hey, Mike, I'm out at my father's, I'm takin' care of my father. He had that hip- replacement surgery." He said, "My sister went on vacation and I'm out here takin' care of him and she didn't leave me no freakin' food!"

So I couldn't get through to Long Island, and I called his machine in Manhattan and left a message. Anyhow, we never spoke again. That haunted me for a long time.

DONALD POOLE – West Palm Beach Firefighter/Paramedic
I was a professional boxer at the time, training at Gleason's Gym, and this guy'd be on the same heavy bag, at the exact same time, every single day. He wore a FDNY T-shirt, so I asked him if he was a firefighter. After that, I never talked to him about boxing, just firefighting. And I never knew that he was the highest-decorated firefighter in the history of the department; he never came across as anybody that thought he was anything more than anyone else.

I was always interested in pursuing my athletic abilities more than my intellect, but Patty encouraged me, convinced me to go to school, get my education, and start putting in applications to different fire departments. So I ended up moving to Florida, and wore a Rescue 2 T-shirt he gave me to classes, every day. I got certified as a Firefighter/EMT, and the last place that I put my application in, I got hired.

The northern tip of West Palm Beach is really vicious and violent—it's not handguns, but AK-47s and cut-you-in-half bullets. And yet, there are people walking this earth today because of Patty Brown, and the influence he had on me. Every time I saved somebody, I've said, "Thank Patty Brown you're alive today." I'm talkin' about, for instance, I-95 at 3:00 a.m., and some girl, partially decapitated, with a broken back, a broken neck…and now she's one-hundred percent medically fit, healthy and happy. That I would be there at the right place, the right time, that's the kind of ripple effect he had. Because of just a few words he said, he changed my life. And then changed a lot of other people's lives.

It wasn't a ripple effect, it was a tidal wave.

"The whole course of human history may depend on a change of heart in one solitary and even humble individual—for it is in the solitary mind and soul of the individual that the battle between good and evil is waged and ultimately won or lost."

—M. SCOTT PECK

Journal Entry — April 20, 2004

Walking north from Grand Central, I approached Central Park, ablaze in the glory of a late morning in late April.

Before entering the park, I had a fairly common "celebrity-sighting"— Tony Roberts with graying curly hair, cell phone to ear—and I half-expected the cameras to be rolling for a Woody Allen movie. I flashed back to 1972 when *Sugar*, the Broadway musical adaptation of the Billy Wilder movie classic, *Some Like It Hot*, was one of the matinees I indulged in between waitress shifts on West 45th Street. Roberts played the Tony Curtis character, and Robert Morse played Jack Lemmon's. Ironically, I have no idea who played the title character, immortalized in film by Marilyn Monroe—the Broadway counterpart now a sugar substitute long-dissolved in the haze of memory. Pat might have been wading through the Cam Lo River or dodging sniper fire while I was safely nestled in my rear balcony theatre seat. In 1972, we were worlds apart.

I wandered into the park from the west side, past waves of daffodils and grape hyacinths, under puffy clouds of pink and white blossoms—

practical thoughts popping into my walking meditation as I noticed how nice a ground cover myrtle made with its blue blossoms punctuating the green; might it be good on the slope next to my driveway? I wound around the Great Lawn, heading toward Pat's tree.

Should Pat die, his brother Mike had his wishes in writing—one of which was to have his ashes spread within view of the city skyline that rose above the Great Lawn like some vast tiara. Central Park was indeed "Patty's Park," an oasis for him that separated Harlem from home—where he ran, bicycled, and occasionally nabbed a mugger. When Pat's remains were still not recovered in November 2001, Mike decided instead to plant a tree where the ashes would have been scattered. It is a young sugar maple, now growing stronger and more assured in the setting behind the Metropolitan Museum, under the watch of Alexander Hamilton's statue. It overlooks an area of lawn where young women like to sunbathe on days like today. Pat would have appreciated this view as well.

60 MINUTES II – September 4, 2002 (transcript excerpt)
The remains of only two men from Ladder 3 were recovered by November. With no bodies to bury, they had memorial services for the ten others—the last one for Captain Paddy Brown. Brown was a Fire Department legend. His specialty: pulling people out of burning buildings. Firefighters heard him reporting on September 11 that Ladder 3 was trying to rescue people somewhere around the fortieth floor of the north tower.

Says Firefighter Mike Moran: "Paddy had pretty detailed instructions if he should ever die in a fire what he wanted done. He had his place in Central Park picked out where he wanted his ashes spread. And his brother Mike was kind of disappointed that we hadn't found his body, that we couldn't fulfill this—it seemed like his only real wish, like what he wanted done. So the next best compromise he felt was if we could plant a tree in his honor. So, we kind of had a stealth mission in the middle of the night, to go plant a tree."

Journal Entry – December 30, 2001

His ashes have been distributed, and I ride home on the train with Pat's security blanket over my lap, warming and protecting me with an emotional intensity so deep I blink tears.

We all met at Frank E. Campbell's Funeral Home, maybe twenty family members and friends. Mike told us the deal: we walk to the park to the spot designated in the will—and we carry out Pat's wishes. And so we stood in the clear cold with Mike walking down the line, offering up the sacrament of Pat's ashes. We scooped down in the bag and held him close one last time, then on cue: "God bless Paddy Brown!" We let him go into the air behind us to join the celestial backdrop of his sparkling city skyline, with black tree branches etched over a glowing full moon.

I was set to go home, but something compelled me to join the living, as most of the crowd was going to the Adriatic. The small, unpretentious restaurant behind his neighborhood pizza parlor had become Pat's own "personal" kitchen, where he'd have pasta with marinara and salad and Diet Coke. In the warmth of garlic-infused air and our group's bizarrely intimate communion, I asked Donny, the cousin who was staying in Pat's apartment, about the blanket. He knew exactly what I was referring to. "That white ratty old thing that's held together by safety pins?" Yes. That was what I wanted. I had earlier asked about but never retrieved the personal gifts I had made him—a hand-painted cereal bowl to "NY's Bravest and Grumpiest," a nude back-view sketch that had perched on the piano. Instead, I am content to have some things that made him feel safe. His Zen- meditation bench, the ski hat he slept in, and most of all, his blanket. I didn't feel like a scavenger, but an archivist—one who would take care of the things that once took care of Pat.

CAROL SHUFRO – Author's Friend

E-Mail to Author

Subject: Closure

Date: December 31, 2001 6:32:18 PM Eastern Standard Time

Sharon,

I want to thank you for keeping me informed of all the tributes and events in honor of Pat. Somehow I have felt that this was my personal connection amidst the mourning of the tragedy on a larger scale. When they speak of the heroes, I hone in on the man I met and who was a part of your life. He captured the hearts of so many people.

Now I understand why you have been so involved in his afterlife. He has truly become a part of all of our lives, beyond the scope he ever imagined.

Pat will keep on saving lives and will keep putting out our eternal and emotional fires, rescuing us and teaching us. He had made his mark in this world alive, and now he lives as a symbol of someone who faced his demons and kept on growing and learning and taking on challenges in such a humble way.

He truly lived in and left this world as profoundly and brilliantly as the full moon on the night his ashes were spread.

Happy 2002——

Love, Carol

Journal Entry – May 7, 2004

I had a rendezvous with Frank today. Twice, now, he has met me on the corner of Seventh and Bedford in the Williamsburg section of Brooklyn, an artsy neighborhood just a few blocks from the gritty waterfront and the Con Edison trailer he operates out of as construction manager. From there, I can see straight across the East River practically into the window of what was Pat's bedroom. We go to a bar, have drinks and an appetizer, smile at each other, flirt a little, and talk. Always, we talk about Pat.

Frank and I started to bond a year after 9/11 at a dedication along the East River outside Stuyvesant Town. The Captain Patrick J. Brown Walkway is part of the beautification efforts that were long under construction eleven stories beneath Pat's bedroom window. The roar of FDR Drive traffic competes with the Zen of sitting by the river, and bikers and runners like Pat can now go for miles with gardens instead of traffic cones punctuating their peripheral vision. Only the flow of the river remains unchanged.

Frank is seriously and existentially curious, putting puzzle pieces together of his childhood friend. He asks many questions, and I try to answer them, as much for myself as for him. He seems to feel that if Pat and he had reconnected and compared their mutual passion for running, that an adult friendship could have blossomed out of the cracks of that Queens Village sidewalk they had once shared. I tend to agree, because the intimacies of childhood are tilled in the purest of soil. Frank wants to go back into his recent past, to 1991, when he last saw his boyhood pal, and weed the plot that surrounded Pat of anything that had the potential of choking or preventing growth. With hindsight, he sees what could have been, and that gives him both comfort and pain.

As for Frank and me, we have become closer in what initially was a "jazzy/casual" way—a phrase I use to describe his speech pattern and Queens accent. At times, it's like scat-talk, but then on a dime, it can turn and connect very deeply and succinctly to my emotional circuits. Frank is married, a family man, a workaholic, a Catholic. Does he sense the things I think I want him to understand, but will not say? I thought our spark was caused by our mutual connection to Pat, and maybe it was, but by now we've established a routine, mostly e-mail, with which I wake up to and start my day. "Frank in the AM" is the subject head. He seems to enjoy his small efforts toward making me happy.

And so, am I?

FRANK BENDL

The first thing that pops into my mind about Patty Brown is "baseball." Patty and I played a *lot* of baseball together when we were kids. Patty played second and I played shortstop, and our dads were both the managers of the team. We played for our school team, St. Joachim and Ann, and we also played in the Hollis-Bellaire-Queens Village Little League. We spent a lot of time together and we had a lot of fun.

We went to grammar school together from the first to the eighth grade, and we kind of hung around on weekends, every weekend. Me,

Patty Brown, and another fella, Richie Engel, were inseparable.

Some of the mischievous things that we did were like jumpin' from garage roof to garage roof down the block, sneakin' in people's basement windows, and stealin' their milk when it was delivered in the milk box. Right before we graduated from grammar school, we happened to go over to the rectory of St. Joachim and Ann and found the door open, so we walked in and took the elevator up to the roof and got out. We were yellin' to everybody in the schoolyard. Well, guess what? The nuns locked us up on the roof; we couldn't get off until they called our parents. So we were all in a heap of trouble there.

The nuns had a hard time controllin' us; we were a little proactive in everything we did. It was at the time of the President Kennedy Physical Fitness thing that came to the schools. They took groups of students and put a leader in charge of every ten kids. Since they couldn't control us, the best thing they could do was make us leaders. We felt like kings. The nuns knew we were mischievous, and I think they liked that about us.

When I used to come over and look for Patty, and if I couldn't find him at home, my first stop was two blocks away, at the firehouse.

If I was gonna think of one word to describe Patty, it would be "unselfish." If Patty had a quarter, you had half of it. If you needed a quarter, Patty gave you his. It was like that with everything. Patty never thought about himself, and I see that now, after all these years. I see who he was and what he was.

Patty and I were real good ball players. One year he didn't make the all-star team, and I did, and he was pretty upset. The big game was played in Brooklyn, and I was up to bat early in the game, and as I got up I hear, "C'mon, Frankie!" I turned around and Patty was behind the cage. He had made his father drive him to Brooklyn and showed up to root me on. But that was Patty.

I guess he forged everything he did later on from those years. Patty went through a lot of things when he was young, and you wind up hearing about it, or realizing it later, the things that he went through that you really didn't grasp at the time. Patty had a lot of different facets to him and his life. I was fortunate to know him when he was so young, and see him turn into the legend that he was, and is. But there are so many reasons why he turned out the way he did.

All the way down, through the layers, were his spirituality, his anger, and the burning desire to help people. I attribute so much to his early years and what he went through, growing up. He was off to the service at seventeen and put in the position to fight for his life. And that tapped into his anger, which also probably was the only reason he could do it, could go to war.

I know he had a bad reaction ("Baby killer!") from people when he returned from Vietnam, and that hurt him a lot because that's not Patty. He really didn't have a mean bone in his body, *at all*. The time he went to war, the times he boxed——I think he was in a position where the anger was coming out of him, the only thing that could get him to do those things in the first place.

When I look at Patty after all these years and everything that transpired, I search my soul for how he became who he was. I think he forfeited so many things in life, because of the person he was. And yet, all the things that he went through made him a better fireman, a better partner, a better brother, a better human being. I don't think you could have given him any other job in life but to save lives. It's just pretty unbelievable that he became who he was, but it doesn't surprise me.

Carolyn was showing me all Patty's medals and all his letters and commendations and stuff, and my first reaction was, How did he have the time to fit all that into forty-eight years? Award, after award, after award—which he unselfishly gave to some charity of his. And I'm sure Patty could have used it, but money wasn't an issue with him. I left bewildered and shaking my head. Where did he find the time to do this? Where did he find the time to be such a hero? When did he grow into such a hero? He is as special as special can be. I could live a lifetime and never meet another person like Patty Brown.

I work for Con Ed, and we interface quite a bit with the fire department, so I'd meet quite a few firemen through different emergencies and schooling, as well as through my kids' activities. And probably fifteen to twenty times after 9/11, I would run into someone who was an older fireman, and I'd introduce myself. I'd say, "I have to ask you a question. Do you know Patty Brown?"

And it's the same reaction, every single time, absolutely, without a doubt, one hundred percent. Everybody smiles and says, "Patty Brown. Of course, I knew Patty Brown."

"Tell me what you're thinking about him, right now," and they all would laugh, and you could see their minds wandering, and it was great to see. Their eyes would go someplace else, their minds would go someplace else, and they'd think of a story, a personal story. And you could see them reminiscing about some great times with a guy they loved, and everybody had a great story.

It was all pretty much the same: "Boy, he was crazy!" "Man, he was great." "God, he was a good guy." "What a fireman!" Never, *ever* a bad word about Patty.

Journal Entry — May 12, 2004

"Rough Road" the sign says as I enter or leave my town on Route 9-D, the road to the train station. There are also a lot of deer crossing warnings posted, largely in vain. I couldn't bear the agony of colliding with one, nor the irony, not after Pat's gift to me that Christmas of 1995 of a vintage Georg Jensen pin. The silver doe is kneeling on her front legs, contained in an exquisite oval composition. Is she stumbling, or just in transition? Her ears are alert, and she looks behind her. I feel that way a lot.

I am on the 11:02, returning from an evening spent at my former therapist's cabaret act. I love the fact that Barbara, the woman to whom I entrusted the reins of my psychological growth some twenty years ago, now considers me a friend and invites me to this other side of her life. The evening moved me in many ways, firstly by her warmth and humor and passion. But also there was an awareness of the bittersweet passing of time since Pat and I sat in her office in an attempt to stop the unraveling of our future together.

The short walk through Times Square to Grand Central was warm and muggy, and the weight of the atmosphere also included the enormity of missing Pat tonight. I cut through the haze and through all the happy loving couples and families—those perplexing people who live on the other side of the pane of glass that Pat and I once pressed our noses against and thought we could join.

On the train, I put on my jacket, polish the pin with the shirttail of my blouse, and wonder how he came to choose such a perfect gift.

BARBARA WAXENBERG

I knew Pat only through his torment and refusal to allow himself to believe that he could be truly loved, as he was by you. I've always thought of him in the biblical words, "a man of sorrows and acquainted with grief."

Journal Entry – May 12, 2004, *continued*

I really didn't know who Pat "was" in the fire department when I first started seeing him. His modesty was overwhelming, with nothing false about it, whatsoever. As we sat talking on my couch, he brought up the topic of his "sorta unusual career." I got a *Cliff's Notes* version that night, including his admission to having a "kinda knack" for locating victims. Later on, as we got to know each other better, he referred to this knack as a type of sixth sense and admitted that he had access to that dimension. My interpretation is that it is a zone where sensitivity and empathy seek out pain, or perhaps the other way around. And that the only thing for Pat to do was: Feel. Act. Rescue. Beyond the practical explanation to others that it was "Location, location, location," he knew that in his case it was more.

Pat sensed presences—his long dead mother at the foot of the bed, a recently killed friend on a gurney. I was a little spooked, a little dubious, and a little envious. But I never doubted his reality.

WANDA SHADWICK

He always sensed everything. He always "knew." He definitely had this "thing."

GEORGE MENAR

Me and Patty went to see *The Towering Inferno*. The next day, there was a fire at the WTC, on two different floors. We, the Fire Patrol, were there—stuck in between. We didn't have air then, but the firemen had Scott packs that were ringin' and goin' off, and guys were running out of air.

So many times we went running into buildings—we'd try and beat the fire department, get a grab, save someone. One time we went to a job and the fire department was there, and we had to fight our way up the stairs, get through the lines that were all over, like spaghetti. We got to the floor above the fire, which was filled with smoke. But there were kids there, and we pulled them down. Patty seemed to know how to find them, too. He had a sense where they were. And that's without goin' to probie school yet, where they teach you that kind of stuff. But he had a little somethin' extra, there.

ARTIE WILLIAMS — Fire Patrol 1
CARLOS RIVERA — Fire Patrol 1

AW: When Patty first came on the Fire Patrol, I was one of the first guys to really get close to him. He looked very young. I mean, when he walked through the door, I said, "How'd this guy get on the job?" Because he looked about sixteen.

We did a lot of drinkin', you know, I mean, outside the job. We marched in the St. Paddy's Day parade, things like that. He always lost his hat—we *all* did! He was always laughing. Always a happy-go-lucky guy. There's a lot of stories—craziness!

CR: You were guaranteed a date whenever you walked with Patty Brown on St. Paddy's Day.

AW: He had a lot of girls after him. He was a good-lookin' guy! But a lot of "girl things" he kept to himself.

CR: He wasn't a player, in other words.

AW: Everything on his mind wasn't "girls girls girls." But he did have girlfriends.

CR: This was like high school. Or "F Troop." Patty would get together with another guy that used to be on this job, George Menar. These guys were like nitro and glycerin. When you combined them together—holy mackerel! One day they just decided, "Let's see who can make the biggest dent on the refrigerator." They would run from this wall, head first, into the refrigerator. First George, then Patty Brown, with his head down, at a full gallop into the thing—BOOM! He dented the thing by about three inches! He was bleeding!

"That didn't hurt!" Then his famous laugh—"Heh, heh, heh, heh!"

It was basically a high school, for all of us at that time. It was pure bedlam.

AW: He always had cars that were forty-dollar throw-away cars. I used to do a lot of work on them; he didn't know much about cars. I don't think he was mechanically inclined.

CR: He was *not* Bob Vila.

AW: He had a car with no front windshield in it. So you can imagine him drivin' down the street.

CR: Remember when he'd park, he'd "clean" the windshield? We said, "There *is* no windshield!"

Patty: "Heh, heh, heh!"

AW: He was a "gung ho" guy. It's not that we don't *do* it, but we usually don't go in and save people at a fire. When we went out on a run, Patty would come sliding down the pole, and he'd be, like, acting. "Come *on*, let's *go*! Let's *go*, guys!"

CR: And we'd go, "All right, Patty, we're going; don't worry about it."

He'd take the pole; everybody else'd take the stairs.

AW: Just jokin' around——"Come on, this is the *big* one; let's *go!*" They were the days when we were really busy, too; the fire department was busy.

We'd get off from here, go have a few beers—but we never got in bar fights, it wasn't like that. It was friendship.

CR: The mesh, the mesh of the personalities. And everyone was about the same age.

AW: He was a good guy; we were all good guys. You'd never see him argue with anybody. Never a violent guy.

CR: As I said, this was "F Troop," and Patty Brown would start a lot of the water fights here. So bad that you'd have to use a pump to get it off the floor—a good two inches or more. We had a chauffeur who looked like Louie DaPalma in *Taxi,* or more like a Joe Pesci——that attitude, always had a cigar. And this guy was related to Joe Costello of the Genovese family. And he would be loading the covers in there, Patty Brown would be upstairs, and instead of just sprinkling water, he would get a waste-basket full, and he'd yell Steve's name. Steve would look up, and all of a sudden, you'd see his legs go out from under him, and there was this bucket of water hitting him on the head. And you would hear that laugh. "Heh, heh, heh, heh!" Then I'd take off and hide in the truck, because I knew the water fight was on.

It was about 6:00 or 7:00 a.m. (May 25, 1977). I had the morning watch, and Jimmy Coyle, Patty Brown, George Menar, and Danny Nastro were working. It came over the radio as a 10-75, a really big fire, in a male bath house with "numerous patrons running out," and they literally just had towels around themselves. We went into the fire, to throw the canvas covers, but our guys were also bringing people out. Patty Brown found two guys passed out from smoke inhalation, in a swimming pool. He did CPR on them, and they were brought back to life. Patty was, like, a big thing there—all the guys were amazed how he was running back and forth.

Jimmy Coyle came back that day, and he says, "Patty saved a lot of people."

AW: He came here one night; it was the middle of the night, and I was upstairs sleepin', and he was in his Marine uniform, and he sat on the end of my bed. I think he had just gotten out of boot camp, and he was talkin' to me about Vietnam. I knew he was a little tipsy, so I said, "Look, Patty, take your uniform off and lay in the bed; we'll talk about it in the morning." So the morning came and as I came down, his father walked through the door.

He says, "Where is he?"

"He's upstairs; I'm bringing him some coffee." He went upstairs, and the next thing I know is they're gone.

I think he was a little worried, like anybody would be, and he wanted somebody to talk to. I didn't really get a chance. He didn't have to join, but he went there, four years. He knew what the consequences were by joining; he knew he was going to Vietnam. I guess he had it in his mind more or less that that's what he wanted to do.

When he came back, he did get quiet, and everything he did was more by himself.

CR: Never, never, never, *ever* did he talk about Vietnam. And nobody asked him. The big thing they told you right away: Don't wake up Patty. If you gotta wake him up, yell at him or throw something at him, but stay away from the bunk. Or he would come out fighting. He was still asleep! Then he'd just wake up gradually.

"I did that? Who did I do that to?" Then, "Heh, heh, heh."

AW: After he got out of the Marines, he came back here, and he took the test for the fire department. He had a hard time getting on because he had eye problems.

CR: He was near-sighted and had astigmatism.

AW: He went to a specialist who had him do eye exercises, and he finally passed and went on and became one of the best, most decorated firefighters this city ever had.

CR: Once he got on the fire department, we'd see him at jobs. He would just happen to be walking by, and we're there, and he'd go, "Have an extra helmet? Have a coat?" and he'd run in. He never forgot where he came from, where his roots are. Even when he was in 26 Truck up in Harlem, he would come down here to run, or to work out at Gleason's Gym. He always made a point to stop in here. Always.

I was watching the six o'clock *Eyewitness News*, and before the commercial break, they say "Daring Rescue in Midtown," and I go, "Eh, big deal." I walk away, and when I come back, I look, and they're showing the guy on the tenth floor standing on the window sill.

"Damn, he looks familiar. Oh my god, it's José!" I said, "That's the guy who used to play in the band with me. I don't believe this!" And then they're showing how they rescued him, and they show Patty Brown!

I said, "I don't *believe* this! My friend's in the window, and my friend saves him!"

Then I get a phone call from the drummer in the band: "I just saw José on the tenth floor; he was about to jump!"

I said, "I know; Patty Brown rescued him!" He rescued the piano player in our band.

And that's when he got in trouble with the fire department, because they had nowhere to tie the rope, so Patty improvised. It was against procedure, and then what happened, to add fuel to the fire—

AW: —was that he talked to the press. And there's a rule in the fire department that you don't give out interviews in your uniform. And then I think that you have to get permission. And he voiced his opinion; he said things they didn't wanna hear.

CR: Cause they did a follow-up, and he was right.

AW: He was right, but it didn't matter. He didn't get any charges or anything—

CR: They couldn't do anything against him because he saved the lives of two people. When the news did the follow-up story, they had Rescue 1 on the roof, and Patty Brown says, "Look around. No where to tie the rope."

AW: He coordinated the whole rescue—

CR: —using snap judgment, for the betterment of the people in distress. And then he said a couple more things, and that's when the whole trouble started, the snowball effect...

AW: He was bein' interviewed about "if we had the right equipment" and stuff like that, and the mayor, David Dinkins, heard, and it became political.

CR: He was then told basically, You'll never work in a Rescue company again.

AW: If you knew him, you knew he was gonna do what he did. There was no hesitation. That's the way he was. He didn't have to prove nothin' to anybody.

JOSÉ GALLEGOS

During the rescue, Patty didn't follow procedure. They had to have a pole or something where the rope had to be tied. I happened to be around the firehouse when somebody was talking about that. He was a high-ranking official in the fire department, and I told him, "Look, whoever wrote the book had all the time in the world to think about the procedures. Pat didn't have time to think. If he would have stopped to think about the book, I would have died. Now how would you feel about that?" And I remember that the man turned pale. He didn't say a word.

FOX 5 Evening News – March 3, 1992 (lead story)
Anchorman: One of New York's most decorated firefighters is behind a desk tonight, taken away from saving lives, and pushing pencils. He's being punished for what he said last night on the 10:00 News.
Penny Crone: Early this morning, Lieutenant Patty Brown was disciplined and transferred from active firefighter duties with Rescue 1 to a desk job. The action came after Brown talked exclusively to FOX 5 News last night and invited Mayor Dinkins to visit with our city's firefighters.
Pat Brown (video footage): Come down to the firehouse; come down

and talk to me, come down and talk to the men; you're invited. No politics, no histrionics, but I wanna tell ya the story.

Penny Crone: Brown's comment was part of a FOX exclusive series concerning rampant discontent within fire department ranks—charges of under-manning on the trucks, antiquated equipment, and budget cuts.

Richard Brower – U.F.O.A. (United Fire Officers Association) President (video footage): Every time they want a hero, they trot Patty Brown out. Every time they wanna show rescues, they trot Patty Brown out. But Patty Brown speaks from the heart, off-duty, and they punish him. And they're not gonna punish Patty Brown as long as we're around.

Penny Crone: One official told FOX 5 News that Patty Brown was not only a fire department hero, but a decorated war hero, and a well-liked and highly respected man.

FOX 5 Evening News – March 8, 1992

Penny Crone: Since his transfer, Brown has had nothing to say, but late this afternoon he expressed his relief.

Penny Crone (video footage): I don't know if you're allowed to talk.

Pat Brown (video footage): (Laughing) Yeah, this time I'm allowed to talk. We talked to Chief Feehan for about an hour, and he's a fine gentleman and we came to a great understanding, and tomorrow I'm back to Rescue 1, thanks to you, thanks to Channel 5, and (looking and smiling at the camera) thank you, everybody that called.

Penny Crone: After a series of reports on Brown's transfer, City Hall and Fire Department headquarters were deluged with calls in favor of Brown. Tomorrow, Brown goes back to his old job.

PAT BROWN – Quote on desk pad at Ladder 5
We are not in charge, we are just responsible.

Journal Entry

Pat had an interesting perspective on his career, especially by the time he settled into 3 Truck in 2000. One day he went down to FDNY headquarters in Brooklyn to see the commissioner about reversing seats in the tower ladder. Many of the units were complaining that riding backward left them unable to prepare for what they were responding to. Commissioner Von Essen agreed and was changing seats selectively, mostly based on the captain and his troops.

As he approached the commissioner's office, he got some ribbing from people he passed in the hallway:

"You in trouble again, Patty?" A seed was planted. He took care of the business at hand with the commissioner, and then decided to put on a little show.

"Act like you're pissed off at me," he coached Von Essen, and after a bit of play-acting between two old friends, Pat skulked out of the office, convincing the onlookers and eavesdroppers that Patty Brown was indeed in the doghouse with the brass, yet again.

Another time, he handed me an article from the *Daily News.* "Look at this," and he went into his bathroom to shower.

New York Daily News – Mike Daley – June, 1999

REV TO STARS GETS SINGED IN SCANDAL

In further proof of the Almighty's affection for irony, the Rev. Pete Jacobs now stands at the epicenter of a $350 million insurance scandal that came to light as a result of a house fire.

Jacobs has long harbored a special fondness for firefighters. He performed the last rites for several of the 12 who died at the 23rd St. fire in 1966, and he apparently decided that those who routinely risk such dangers should not also have to worry about the fires of hell.

Accordingly, he years ago introduced the city's firefighters to a novel concept in the absolution of sin.

"He'd say, 'I absolve you of all your sins in the future,'" Fire

Capt. Pat Brown recalls. "His thinking was, 'God knows the things you're going to do in the future and you're going to be sorry for them, so I'll absolve you now.'"

Jacobs bestowed his special forgiveness on everyone present at a Rescue 1 dinner in the early 1980s.

"The more conservative Catholic guys were like looking at each other," Brown says. "Guys like me were eating it up."

As this was that time before AIDS dampened the city's nightlife, Brown was not alone in finding Jacobs' brand of absolution particularly handy. Brown's favorite spots included Da Silvano's restaurant and he often encountered Jacobs there. Jacobs demonstrated that he also had a special fondness for celebrities.

"He was wherever the big shots were," Brown says.

Jacobs' saving grace was that he would act as if he were only introducing equals when he presented Brown to the likes of Paloma Picasso. Jacobs repeatedly invited Brown to fly off to Europe with him.

"He'd say, 'You want to go to Monaco? We'll see the princess and hang out. And then we'll go to the Vatican. I've got a couple of friends there. We'll go see the Pope. We'll get you a private audience,'" Brown remembers.

And, Jacobs really did have prominent friends at the Vatican and among the royals of Monaco. His other buddies included Walter Cronkite and Gloria Steinem. He maintained five phone lines and carried a beeper that once sent him dashing off from a dinner party. He returned and opened his hand to show *Ms.* magazine publisher Patricia Carbine six bullets, saying he had just saved someone from committing suicide.

In December 1982, Jacobs opened his own restaurant, Palatine, on W. 46th St. He announced that all profits would go toward scholarships at Power Memorial Academy and Rice High School, where he served as chaplain. He was nonetheless ordered to desist by the Archdiocese of Washington, D.C., where he had been ordained.

He ignored the edict, and each night the place filled with celebrities and firefighters. The patrons looked up from their rabbit en aspic one night to see Brown and another firefighter dash out to rescue a man from a blaze across the street. On another evening, Jacobs introduced Brown to a countess.

"He said, 'He works up by where Jackie lives,'" Brown says.

Jackie being Jackie Onassis, who lived on Fifth Ave. Brown was assigned to a firehouse up at 115th St. "But, it was Fifth Ave.," Brown says.

Jacobs still had prominent Vatican connections that dated to the early 1960s, when he assisted Pope John XXIII's efforts to bring the church closer to the Jewish community. Jacobs had been particularly suited to this task, as his father was Jewish.

The lure of those connections was apparently what prompted a man who called himself David Rosse to make Jacobs the president of the St. Francis of Assisi Foundation last summer. Jacobs invited Cronkite to serve as an adviser, saying the foundation would be giving $1 billion to the poor. Cronkite demurred, but he was listed as an adviser anyway.

On May 5 of this year, the Greenwich Fire Department responded to a report of a fire at a $3 million house in that Connecticut town. The firefighters discovered piles of records ablaze.

The St. Francis of Assisi Foundation proved to be a ruse designed to prop up a pyramid scheme whereby Rosse siphoned at least $335 million from insurance companies.

Jacobs insists he was simply a dupe, and Brown is among those who believe him. Brown also figures that the absolution still holds.

"As far as I'm concerned, I'm good the rest of my life," Brown says.

Journal Entry, *continued*

He came out of the shower wearing a grin as he saw me scrutinizing the article, trying to comprehend just what it might mean. I was exasperated. "Pat, how are you gonna get Rescue 1 if you keep ending up in things like this?" But he just cackled. And finally, now, I can see the humor in it that he saw all along.

Above: John "Persh" Brown, Pat and Mike, October, 1963.

Right: Pat, Richie Engle, and Mike, Queens Village.

Above: Boot camp
(Pat, left) at Parris
Island, 1970.

Left: In Nam,
3rd Marine Division.

Right: Golden Gloves contender training at Gleason's Gym.
Photo credit: James Malcolm

Below: In a hospital bed while a probie with Ladder 26.

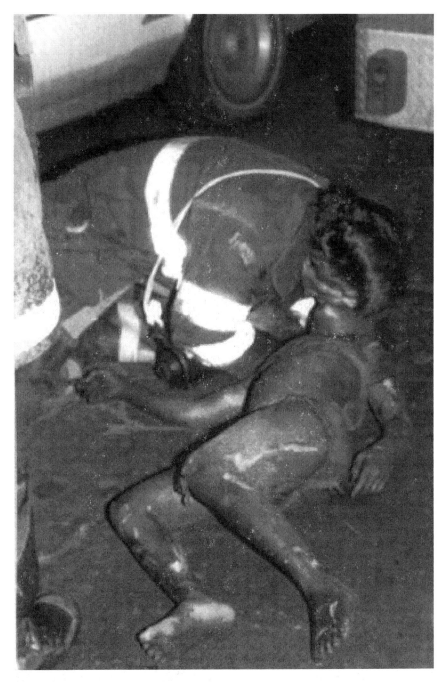

Opposite page: After a job in Brooklyn, Rescue 2.

Above: Administering mouth-to-mouth.

Photo credit: Harold W. Doyle

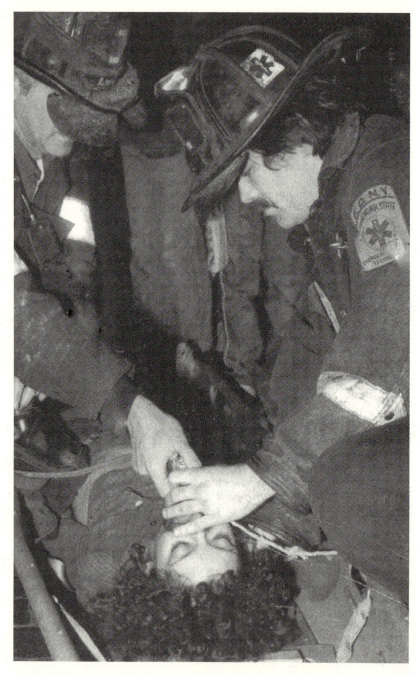

Above: Pat and another Rescue 1 firefighter resusitatiate a young woman.
Photo Credit: NY Daily News

Opposite page: Pat lowers Kevin Shea down the rope to rescue second victim in Times Square, May 1991. *Photo Credit: Michael Norcia, NY Post*

Opposite page: A pensive Pat at home.

Right: Sharon and Pat at Brown family home in Westbury, NY, December 1995.

Below: Pat and Sharon at the Grand Canyon, January 1996.

Top: St. Patrick's Day, 1996.

Left: Home from the parade.

Opposite page: Pat tackles KP with a smile.

Left: Pat and godson James Coyle relax at Ladder 3.

Below: Pat and Commissioner Von Essen discuss the thermal imaging camera to the news.

Opposite page, top: Pat receives a handshake from Kaicho Nakamura at black belt promotion, February, 1997.

Opposite page, bottom: Pat & Mike Shepherd.

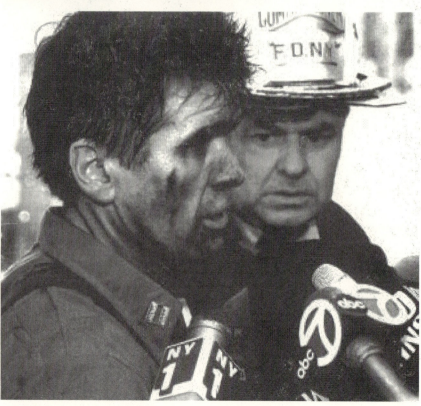

Loving tributes adorn Pat's tree in Central Park.

"There is no greater hatred in the whole world than the hatred of ignorance for knowledge." —————GALILEO GALILEI

Journal Entry – May 19, 2004

The 9/11 Commission has come to NYC, televised live, and I see that the wound is still so raw for so many. Family members who lost their loved ones sit in the auditorium and their anger and frustration erupts—biting, it seems at times, the hand that is feeding them. It was they who were left to mourn, galvanized by the four widowed wives from New Jersey, to persevere and press the stubbornly secretive Bush administration to form the investigative panel. Now they react to former Mayor Giuliani, demanding tougher questions from the panel, demanding explanations for the communication problems (technical and human), demanding any shred of information that will provide a balm to their pain. I empathize and yet know we are all looking through a rear-view mirror. We know the outcome, and we want to change what led up to it. We want to re-roll the tape, start over, and fix it.

I think when all is said and done, there will be accountability in all departments and at every level. Mayor Giuliani was extraordinary in his ability to keep us as calm and sane as humanly possible in those days and weeks following 9/11, both individually and as a nation. I feel badly for the people whose pain has not metamorphosed into some kind of rooting soil for healing. Yes, we need answers. Yes, accountability vindicates our pain and anger somewhat. But assigning blame, like exacting revenge, is not a true and lasting satisfaction.

This morning, the mayor described what he personally experienced that morning. He acknowledged the FDNY's caliber of excellence, and loss. Hearing Pat's name stopped me mid-brushstroke at my art table. I am reminded that I am one whose wound is still not closed.

RUDY GIULIANI – Former New York City Mayor – *9/11 Commission Report*

People exited this building carefully, they exited this building quickly, they exited this building without harming or hurting each other. And the credit for that goes to Pete Ganci and Bill Feehan and Terry Hatton and Patty Brown and Mychal Judge, and I wish I could mention all the firefighters and the police officers; those happened to be the ones that I saw that morning, right before they died.

THOMAS VON ESSEN

They did a good job with the 9/11 Report. I mean, I hated the politics and the pandering of the committee up on the stage, but the people behind the scenes who wrote it did a good job. The phonies with agendas, up on the stage, were kind of upsetting—the politics of some of the questions and the way they came after the fire department. They knew there was no reason to go after us, but they felt like, the families are here; let's rip them up.

That's the worst thing I think you can do—and so many people in the department have done it, and so many politicians have done it—is make the family think that something was handled wrong. The guys didn't do anything wrong. They're in a battle, mistakes get made, things that, if you looked the next day, you'd do differently. These are the finest chiefs in the world, operationally, the most experienced, the most dedicated, and they didn't think that the buildings were gonna come down that fast, period.

PERIOD. Now, if the best chiefs in the world thought, "Holy shit, these buildings are gonna come down in one-hundred and two minutes," and you're sending people up to the sixtieth floor, well then shame on you. But if you think that you've got 'til 8:00 p.m. tonight until these buildings come down—that's a different story.

I couldn't mislead a mother or a widow like that. If we screwed up, you tell them, and if we didn't, you don't lead them down that path— "blame this, blame that, blame somebody"—instead of just saying it's a tragedy.

Journal Entry – June 23, 2005
The walk down West 43rd Street takes me to the newly christened block: Captain Terry Hatton Way. How many streets, bridges, walkways, parks, and benches have been renamed since the towers fell? This is part of the new world, and while it's nice that Terry has his block and Pat has his walkway, I long for a simpler time.

My wish is almost granted. On the corner, I look past Terry's street sign and into 1963—a pastiche evoking computer graphics more than reality. The zigzag chrome canopy of the Market Diner invites me into a time warp, when the fears of the day were not of jets filled with fuel and suicidal fanatics, but rather of Nikita Kruschev's bellow: "We will bury you!" channeling Sputnik-era anxiety through our black-and-white TV rabbit ears.

The restroom's smell of artificial cherry disinfectant mingled with smoke from a sneaked cigarette break, the plastic pansies stuck in window boxes, the perfect diner iced coffee—all encase me in a sensory bubble and I drift back to 11th Avenue and the reality of the day. I am heading to the Licensing Show at the Javits Center. For my so-called career. There, I am sucked back into the ludicrous banality of the "real world." Technology flagrantly flaunts the leap made from grainy Zenith consoles to digital widescreen. Superheroes still fight Evil, while superheroes with streets named after them are gone.

Who will be remembered? Who are more revered?

———————————

A later-in-life friend of Pat's, who also happened to be a reporter, asked me not too long after 9/11 what I made of Pat's "weird charisma." Even as I inwardly bristled protectively around my memories of him, I knew what she meant.

Like the old folktale of the ten blind Indians feeling an elephant, we were all convinced we knew him best, and we wondered who all these other people were——why were they describing (and how *dare* they?) that which only we knew so well?

Pat's emotional palette had every possible shade, every nuance of value, and with empathetic brushstrokes, he filled in all the frightening spaces that make us feel so alone.

Still, there were times when he was firmly planted in the world of black and white——the values an infant identifies first in a mobile above a crib; at which a child grasps for safety when he learns the world is filled with good and evil; and which an adult feels is a stable foothold in a very shaky world.

"Weird charisma?" Perhaps. Or the aura of one who felt his feelings with such intensity that he made us all feel safe enough to try it on our own.

BERYL BENDER BIRCH —Yogi and Author of *Power Yoga*
As far as I know, I was Pat's first yoga teacher, along with my husband Thom. We taught yoga through the Roadrunners' Club at the Convent of the Sacred Heart School on 91st and 5th in New York City, and some very, very, very good athletes (and I'd include Pat Brown in this group), as well as runners, were taking our classes. By 1995 or so, we had already been teaching this astanga stuff to athletes for fifteen years and we had fifty, sixty, seventy people in every class.

Every once in a while, someone comes into your class whom you notice the first time, and I remember Pat's first yoga class. He was just outstanding. You could see he had an incredible work ethic. He worked at an intense pace. You could see that he was very focused, that he paid attention; he was tuned in. He just had a *prana*, an energy about him that was different than most of the people who came through, and you just see that in people occasionally. We call them "old souls," in yoga tradition. Spiritually speaking, he'd been around a long time.

He was tight! Oh my god, was he *tight*! I think after my husband he was the tightest person who ever came to yoga class. His shoulders were like two rocks of Gibraltar. "Pat, touch your toes." "What toes?" Bio-mechanically, from the stress of his work, and his training in the Marine Corps and the FDNY and everything else in his biography, he was a wreck.

Pat was not only tight physically, he was tight psychologically; he was closed down. From a yoga perspective, you would say that the heart chakra was closed; it was very big, it was very full, but it was closed down. It would have taken another ten years with a lot of backward bending to crack open all the pain that he had locked in. In a very real, tangible sense, you could see that he had a tough childhood. Those are the things that people start opening up to, when they start taking yoga—releasing a lot of the old baggage that's stored in the tissue. You start talking; that's the whole opening process, whether it's spiritual, physical, or mental.

I teach and practice a hands-on tradition, so I wrestled with this man in hand-to-hand combat every Monday and Wednesday night. We started on the physical plane and the mental plane, but I think Pat always understood, because it was part of my teaching, that there was a spiritual element that was just beneath the surface, that all this work in asana wasn't just to become more flexible and more injury-free and maybe more focused as a firefighter, but it was also a path to God that was not a religion; it was a scientific methodology that was very compatible with any religious tradition or heritage.

We spent a lot of time talking about the spiritual pathway. We talked about leaning into the discomfort, that life wasn't easy—that life was both birth and death, and gain and loss, and pleasure and pain—that it wasn't one big rollercoaster ride up a hill. Whatever happens is not a mistake. As tragic as it is for those of us who got left behind, and as tragic and painful and beyond any verbal description that the 9/11 episode was for all of us—it still wasn't a mistake. It is a teaching.

Of course, you can't think about that right after the event, because you need time to grieve and recover, and a lot of people are still grieving in far more painful ways than I can even imagine. But at some point, for every soul, you finish, you go on, you ask, "What was my teaching?" What was the teaching for us as a people? Is the teaching really to rush over to bomb Iraq and create more terror and more pain and more suffering? I don't know, but I know that Pat really believed that everything that happens in life can be viewed as a teaching. I think that he really understood the main teaching of yoga, and of the Buddhist tradition as well—that our work here is to help eliminate suffering. And that's why he did what he did; that's why he went into that building, and that's why he wasn't afraid to die. Did he suffer? We want to think that death comes quickly, but suffering happens. Suffering *is*. Who knows if he was ready to die? I know he thought about it, talked about it. Wasn't afraid of it, really. It's amazing the way the mind works—you want to go there; you want to be with him at the moment of his death. What happened? What did he feel? Was he afraid? Maybe it's because we all want to know what it's going to be like; I mean, we're all going to die.

I can remember the night he came to class with a cast on his arm, just after his shoulder surgery. It must have been around 1998. It didn't slow him down at all. And we worked so hard on rehabilitating his shoulder, all the tendons and ligaments. He was determined to reuse that shoulder. He always wanted to take two yoga classes, back to back. I'd say, "Pat, come back later this week. You *don't* want to take two in a row. Come twice." But he always would try and take two in a row, and *did*, often, but half the time I threw him out.

Pat had a special quality; everybody says that and noticed that, but it was true. If he felt that I needed to sit in his car half the night and talk to him about something, he'd sacrifice his sleep just to be available. He really made you feel like you were the only person he ever talked to about his problems, or asked about your problems. I certainly had the impression that I was pretty close to him. He made people feel that way, which is a great attribute. I used to think of him as "CROW" in the Native American tradition—— the people who carry crow medicine are the keepers of sacred law. They are also able to transmute themselves, or what's called in Shamanic tradition, "shape shift."

Shape-shifting means being able to change into any form that you want, so you could appear as a fly on the wall or a coyote in the bush, or you could be two places at once, or you could be telling the same story to one hundred people simultaneously. I always used to think that of Pat— not necessarily literally, that he was able to duplicate himself or manifest in two places at once, but almost. Figuratively, he was able to shape-shift. He was able to change form and connect with people on their own levels. He was able to adjust his frequency, and match impedance levels with whomever he was talking to, and that's a great skill.

I knew immediately when the towers fell that Pat was in there. I don't know how I knew that, but I think that a lot of people who were connected to him knew that he was in there. Just psychically knew.

"He who knows himself best, esteems himself least." ——PROVERB

Journal Entry – June 9, 2004

My car battery is dead. The Beacon taxi service arrived unexpectedly early to take me to the station. Have I grabbed my tape recorder, my FDNY contact notebook, my sunglasses? We are in a mini-heat wave, so rivulets of discomfort seep into my organizational skills. And it's not as if I do this for a living.

Somehow, I have the feeling that I am nearing the mid-point of this project. Or maybe I am being optimistic and it is really more like the three-eighths mark. Still, I am out of the starting gate, and there is no going back. At times I blink in wonder at what I've embarked upon. The net I cast, tentatively at first, then again with new purpose, turns up new avenues, new people, and loses some as well. As names on a list, they are potential sources of information, abstract preconceptions or blanks to be filled in. But when I speak to them by phone, the word "contact" takes on its stickier definition. Now there is a voice, a personality, a history, and an energy behind the name that somehow connects to Pat.

And in the case of Regina Coyle, there is a grieving mother's need. I had known that one of the men lost in Pat's company was a probie, just ten months on the job, and, coincidentally, James Coyle, Jr. was Pat's god-son. I called the Coyle residence in Marine Park, Brooklyn, and left a mes-sage. Sometimes a gin and tonic or glass of wine is required for me to make certain calls, and this was one of those times. Regina, a woman close to my own age bearing a loss I can't even begin to imagine, called me back. Losing James, her oldest child, has her willing or even needing to talk to me and share with me—anything to help keep the memory of her son alive. She pulls my heartstrings and gives me a jumpstart.

REGINA COYLE

It was funny; when James was little, he always wanted to be Luke Skywalker, and we said, "No, you can't be Luke Skywalker." So he says, "All right, then I'll be a fireman." He wasn't a daredevil-type kid; he just liked helping people and he just wanted to be a fireman. He always heard stories of Patty and had that hero worship. He knew that Patty was something special, and he idolized him from the time he was a little boy. There was just something about Patty that he loved.

He had to keep a journal for the job—everything that was technical. In that whole book, this was the only personal thing he had ever written, and it was signed by Captain Brown:

(February 5, 2001) "I have many heroes, too many to mention. I'm just a boy, a little boy—trying to handle the real men that surround me, each and every tour."

Patty got him to take classes at the YMCA—fencing, ballet, and they took a yoga class together. Patty said, "You can't hit on the girls 'til you go at least four times, so they know you're serious." Like Patty, he could do that; it didn't bother him that people might make fun of him—he didn't care. He really just wanted to live every minute.

I remember him sitting there—it must have been the end of August, 2001—and he was trying to connive money out of us. He was going on vacation to Chicago, and he had his tickets for a Cubs football game, and he had his airplane ticket for September 11. And I said, "James, you're gonna be an old man; relax!" And he goes, "Mom, I gotta live every minute of every day." And that's the way he lived. I was lucky he was able to tell me that. He burned the candle at both ends, and it burns out quick, but a lot of flame—and I think he got that from Patty.

After September 11th, I went back to work. I teach young children, and at one point I happened to look at my roll book and the date was March. And I thought, "March? How did I get to March?" I was like sleep-walking for six months. I don't know how I got through every day. I would get up, go to work, come home, and just be wiped out. It was such an unconscious effort just to get through the day. And I said, I can't live like this. James wouldn't want us to be like this. He would want us to live and remember and honor him. try to live every day as a gift from God. I can't change yesterday, but I can take today and live today, and try and be the best person I can. And so that's what I do. It is hard; I never stop thinking of James.

He came to me in a dream, saying he was safe and happy... He was safe and he's happy. And I said, okay, I can live with that.

Journal Entry – June 9, 2004

Lost on Metro North: my talisman—the Harlem Hilton baseball cap Pat gave me when he worked there as Captain of Engine 69. I left it behind on that late night train home, after catching Adam Roth's gig at the Parkside Lounge. I figured if my wallet once turned up in the Lost & Found box, surely my hat would, too. Of no value to anyone, with its faded crown, creased with plaster dust, stained with gardening sweat, having survived a trip to Vietnam and back—no value at all except in priceless sentiment. The box offered nothing, nor did the man in charge of lost articles. No sympathy for a person missing one FDNY hat, navy blue.

ADAM ROTH – Pat's Friend

I met Pat in 1990 at a restaurant. A friend introduced us. I was kinda nervous, 'cause he seemed like a tough guy, and he didn't talk much. I hung out with him a few more times and found him to be a really sweet guy who was actually uncomfortable in the nightlife scene. Yet later in our friendship, we had great times hanging out at sushi joints 'til all hours.

I'm a musician, and he would come see me play gigs all the time. I'd be up on stage beating my brains out trying to attract women, and he would just sit there. After the show, all the girls would ask me, "Who's your friend?" 'Cause he was pretty handsome. Sometimes I'd be walking home with some girl, and he'd pull up in a fire truck and give us a ride. That was a nice thing 'cause it would really impress the chick I was with.

Pat was very funny, yet a lot of his humor was kinda lost on people, I guess because of his delivery. He didn't have great comic timing, but that made him even funnier to me.

We would talk for hours and hours, about everything under the sun. He was very smart, but not cocky about it. The guy was such a tender person, but he wouldn't take any shit, either.

One time he decided after one of my shows to learn piano, so he got one and put it in his apartment. He called me up to go over and teach him a few chords. Well, I showed up, and the piano was a grand piano, and it took up over half of his pad. We had to climb over the thing to even get in the place!

One Christmas he pulled me aside and said he had a present for me. We walked to the trunk of his car, a rusted-out Maverick, and he opened the trunk and gave me a book on Tai Chi. I don't know a lot of firemen, but I don't think they hand out many Tai Chi books for Christmas. He loved being a fireman, and I went to see him at the 13th Street house one time. He was watching some probie mop the floor. I suggested that we get a coffee in the kitchen, but he wouldn't leave the garage. He said he wanted the probie to know that he wouldn't make the guy do anything that he wouldn't do himself.

He came to my wedding; my mother loved him. (Of course, she did; she's a woman!) And I had a message on my machine from him saying he'd come. On the message he said, "Adam Roth getting married! I guess if you can do it, Pat Brown can do it!"

I didn't know about all the things he did for other people. At his funeral I learned. When he hung out with me, I thought I was doing him a favor by getting him out of the house. Now I know that it was Pat who was doing *me* the favor, by giving me his time. He wouldn't have mentioned it 'cause he was pretty humble. As a matter of fact, he might have been the most humble guy I ever met. I really love that guy. Pat Brown was many things to many people, but one thing that he was to all people was a hero.

Journal Entry

Despite or because of Pat's late-in-life passion for yoga, his inner child was very much alive and saying, "Look at me!" I'd visit in that last year we were still seeing so much of each other, 2000... He'd kick up into a handstand on his brand new Tibetan three-by-four-foot prayer rug, his feet touching the sliver of wall that divided the living room from the kitchen with its soy milk-stocked fridge. I still couldn't master that move, but I'd immediately counter with a headstand or a wheel, palms anchored to the old red wall-to-wall carpet. We were like kids in a playground, showing off and sharing our yoga moves in the new millennium.

SEANE CORN

The dialogue between us was really intimate in a lot of ways, because he was so soulful. I couldn't believe that this guy was a fireman. He was an artist. He loved people so genuinely. He was such a character: charismatic, and philosophical, and honest. And vulnerable. I couldn't believe the things that he would talk about, without blinking an eye, about himself. And how he was able to get me to talk about things that I hadn't ever really shared, nor really wanted to, necessarily. But he would just draw that information out.

I moved to Los Angeles and got into yoga very seriously and heard through the grapevine that Pat had gotten into it too. And I always presumed that we would see each other again in this environment, as yogis. I thought, one of these days he'll just show up in my class, just to surprise me.

THOMAS VON ESSEN

I knew about the yoga before September 11th. I used to joke about it all the time. The first year after retiring as commissioner I gave a lot of speeches, talking about how terrific the guys were, and Patty was one of the people I talked about. He had the ability to walk into a firehouse and see a horror like September 11th, and all of a sudden, you've got 11 guys on a truck instead of five, and it's because his leadership was just so strong that these guys would follow him anywhere. And they're going higher than anybody else, and they're going faster than anybody else. All those qualities—strength, leadership, that physical presence and bravery—and then the guy's in a yoga magazine in tights! It takes much more courage in the FDNY to do that than it does to respond to a routine fire. Of course, you're afraid going in, but you're so conditioned to helping people; this is what you *do*, this is what you *love*, and nobody's gonna abuse you for that. But being featured in a yoga magazine, you *absolutely* know the abuse you're gonna get when it becomes published, and you can imagine the editorial comments that are all over it, throughout the firehouse.

JIM WIND – Lieutenant, FDNY Ladder 3 – Excerpt from *Yoga International Magazine* – December, 2001

We all loved Patty. Everyone who knew him did. The yoga meant a lot to him. It helped him get through the painful times, when he lost friends. He was a real open-minded guy. If Patty had a strong opinion about something, it always came from looking at things from here (opening his burly arms as wide as they would reach).

KRISTIN LEIGH – *Yoga International Magazine* – December, 2001

The chanting really hit him. It opened him up and allowed him to release his sadness. I was drawn to him right away and glad to have him in the room. He had metal in his shoulder and knee problems from running marathons and bicycling, but he never balked at any pose. He was committed to the yoga practice, and it was clear he really wanted to be there.

He appreciated whatever spiritual teaching I had to give, and he really listened, even when he came to my class three times in one week and I gave the same talk. He felt like he was in the right place, you could just tell.

KATHERINE PEW — *Yoga International Magazine* — December, 2001

Patrick Brown was one of the most daring and decorated firefighters in the New York City Fire Department, but I never knew it. I knew him as a fellow yogi who faithfully took classes with me at Jivamukti Yoga Center. Even when Pat worked all night, he would come to class first thing in the morning, before going home to bed. When he had two weeks off this past summer, he stayed here in New York's sweltering heat so he could focus on honing his yoga practice.

We were both regulars in the 6:15 evening class. Pat always gravitated toward the back of the room, where he would sit quietly with his legs crossed, waiting for things to begin. If the room was crowded, he was quick to move his mat to make space for others. He never passed me without saying hello, and somehow he knew my name. The last time I saw him was in early September. He was sitting on the ledge of the fountain in the lobby, where he often lingered after class to talk with fellow students and teachers. His hair was slick with sweat, and he was putting on his shoes. "Hi, Katherine," he said. There was something so familiar about him that I asked, "Do I know you from somewhere else?" He smiled. "No, just here." And that was the last I saw of him.

NANCY LA NASA — Founder of Abhaya Yoga Center, Pensacola, Florida
My fondest memory of Pat was from one beautiful spring morning—2001, of course. Just one of those magical New York City days—trees

leafing, birds singing, not too much traffic yet; it felt great to be out. I was heading to the greengrocer on Avenue A in the East Village, ambling along, being lazy, and enjoying a day off from teaching yoga. I saw Pat ride by on his bicycle like I often did, madly going somewhere, always looking very serious and determined. (I always felt kind of dopey around him, his focus was so intense. His was a persona to be reckoned with, yet all the while you felt there was a softer side to him.)

He saw me and slowed down to holler, "Hey, I'm so glad to see you, Nancy! I wasn't going to go to yoga class today, but now that I've seen you, I'm inspired! See you there?"

It certainly puffed me up—that "inspired" bit. And of course, I had to go to yoga class that day, also!

Soon it was September, and we know the rest of the story. A few days after 9/11, I asked my husband if he would walk with me to Pat's firehouse. We just stood across the street and Tom held me and gave me his handkerchief.

Pat radiated something that very few people have. Pat's my hero. Simple.

MARIA RUBINATE – *Yoga International Magazine* – December, 2001

At Jivamukti Yoga Center, when I was teaching from the *Gita* and Pat was in class, I was so humbled. I thought to myself, "What can I teach a guy like this about right action?" He devoted his life to it, and he went out in a blaze of glory, dying in his attempt to serve others. His selflessness was like a beacon of light amid the destruction and despair.

PAT BROWN (about Yoga)

I was really burnt out, you know, emotionally—and it's given me kinda like a solace, an introspection. It's kinda really helped me feel the beauty of life again, you know, when it comes.

Journal Entry – June 16, 2004

This project—it holds me together at a time when my career seems so nebulous. Am I following my bliss, as Joseph Campbell advises on PBS reruns? I try to channel Philippe Petit on a high wire; alone I balance a new roof, the gutting of a bedroom, the monthly mortgage and car payments, with the delicate casting and drawing in of the net filled with stories and memories of Pat.

My pleasures are simple: watering flowers at the start and end of each day, propping my feet up on the front porch rail as I sip a glass of wine. I take in the occasional dog walkers, the flicker of fireflies and television sets, and relish the perfect simplicity of a summer evening.

Preparing for a yard sale, I go through closets, stumbling upon Pat's still freshly pressed and laundered standard-issue FDNY work shirt. That cold, clear night that we distributed his ashes, his friend James and I had the chance to go back to Pat's apartment to claim a few sentimental items. I wanted to give a home to Pat's meditation bench that he had ordered from the artisan who crafted them out of pine for the Zen classes at our karate school. Pat used to kid me that I should meditate more. And so it sits in my meditation corner, where occasionally I put it to use. I keep thinking, Yes, Pat, I will.

As James and I tentatively and reverently walked around that familiar and now hallowed space with the fire engine-red carpet, Donnie (Pat's cousin, who was staying there temporarily) dodged in and out of the periphery of our emotional states, offering up Pat's shoes, shirts, dishware, whatever, almost as if it were a tag sale. In an effort to stop his well-meaning but definitely disconcerting generosity, I think, I chose the blue shirt with the FDNY patch and the navy blue poly/cotton tie with the FDNY-issue tie clip. No captain bars on the collar, but I could see the Braille-like relief where he would pin them. Or rather, I saw that later. Now.

I pull the shirt out of the closet in a perfunctory way, making space, assessing contents. And I notice the cuff. The buttons are misaligned. This officially pressed and laundered officer's shirt, not knowing it was out of service as of September 11, 2001, still holds the imprint of its owner. A miss-buttoned cuff, probably done as Pat quickly dressed one morning, never noticing that the buttons did not line up. The Stuyvesant Town Laundry ironed and sealed that tiny reminder of Pat into a blue shirt, which found its way into my closet inventory. I burst into tears.

JAMES REMAR – Pat's Friend

It is not necessarily appropriate to rate people in this life; after all, who am I to do so?

Nevertheless, if I had to, Pat Brown was the finest man I ever met. He was tough, and he was exceedingly gentle. The last time I saw him was September 6th, 2001. This was at the end of a wonderful summer wherein he and I got to play a lot—talking, going to yoga, eating sushi, and horsing around with my two children. Pat and I hadn't spent so much time together in many years, and to reconnect and revitalize our relationship was and is a great gift.

My daughter Lisa is a gutsy little kid, and Pat adored her. On her bicycle and generally running around, Lisa knows no fear. Pat thought Lisa's boldness and openness and frank manner were wonderful; he admired her honesty and courage. I guess she is a lot like him. My son Jason, of course, was very important to Pat, who was the first person besides myself and healthcare workers and Jason's mom to hold him. Pat was Jason's godfather, and he adored Jason as well.

I had to return to California to go to work on a TV show, and my family and I were saying goodbye to Pat. He was heading toward the elevator in our building, and I said to Lisa, "Go give Uncle Patty a hug." Lisa enthusiastically ran to Pat and jumped into his arms, and they hugged each other. When they let go and Pat said, "Bye, Lisa" there were tears in his eyes—something I had never seen before.

I figured we would all be hanging out again soon, but I reflect on that moment and how it felt. I know Pat knew he would be leaving soon, and as painful as this life was for him, he didn't want to go.

Pat loved deeply and completely; maybe that is why he had so many admirers. People felt loved when they were near him. I know my little Lisa did, my Jason, my wife Atsuko did—and I did. As I write this, I still do.

Journal Entry – June 22, 2004

From Grand Central to the Grand Strand——I am off to Myrtle Beach and its healing powers of warm salt water, sunshine, and most important, the comfort that only old high school friends can deliver. I need to walk along the shoreline and allow the sand to pumice my tired, neglected feet, and the salt air to pumice my tired, erratic mind. I need laughter to buoy me above my waves of doubt.

So far, post-9/11 healing has been fueled by the purity of an undiluted, unconditional love for Pat. Not captured in amber—a fossil of love and memory stored in my heart as a relic or souvenir of our sometimes euphoric, sometimes tortured relationship——it is alive and pulses some wonderful and rare energy I was never aware of before, taking me to destinations that surprise me.

This roadmap of healing unfolds further. My project—this collection—is the primary vehicle on the map. It is a bulldozer, a Maserati, a bumper car, a Yugo, a 1986 gold Honda Civic with a rose tucked under the windshield wiper. It plows, detours, takes scenic routes, stops for turtle crossings, picks up hitchhikers, accelerates unexpectedly, grinds to a stop, and gets caught in traffic loops. It goes into the shop for repairs.

There are a few other things in my life that are contributing to my general maintenance, but so far, my vehicle hasn't been nudged aside. I met a guy in town I think I could like. He's in the rearview mirror, and slowly approaching. I wonder if we can share the road.

Is air travel forever robbed of its wondrous aura of adventure? I used to love being checked in at an airport, untethered and free to meander through the gift shops and food kiosks, observing fellow travelers through a lens of imagination and knowing that "real life" was suspended until my return. Anything could happen.

Now I sit at a food court table, eye-level with the taxiing planes. Instead of raring at the gates, they seem lethargic and wounded. Newly designed surroundings at LaGuardia include large orange banners with graphics in a loose brushstroke that I could have done better. They hang with determined cheerful mediocrity in my consciousness, their graphic style as tired as my once romantic notions of air travel. My once buoyant, soaring balloons of anticipation now burst into shreds by box cutters.

Journal Entry – June 27, 2004

Impossibly gorgeous day. Impossibly blue skies. Impossibly. Impossible. Yet there that morning was, arms wide open and full of promise. There that sky was, showing off the city's gleaming shoulders with a cerulean silky shawl of a breeze. And there the impossible happened. Still impossible, it seems to me now as I look up into a replica of that shade of blue. I sit on a granite bench several blocks away that nearly three years ago was blanketed in a toxic, tragic shroud of pulverized cement, and bones, and dreams. Impossible.

This morning, I walked to the site for the first time in two years. The entrance to the PATH train is newly opened, its airy metal canopy swooping and jutting out of the pit in an attempt to welcome and reassure. The observation area surrounding the vast space has transformed into a tasteful grid, with historic photographs and informative descriptions of the entire lifespan of those sixteen acres, engraved into metal plaques. It starts from the earliest settlement days, when Peter Stuyvesant claimed Manhattan for Dutch trade, and continues on with the evolution of the World Trade Center. The names of victims, all called heroes, are listed as well. I can feel Political Correctness settling like fine ash over the modern generic design with its brushed aluminum framework—all in effort to soothe us, and to smooth away the horror so that we are left with matte memories of the impossible.

SIMONE ZAPPA

The first few hours after the towers collapsed, I just wanted Patty to call. But by the next day, I said, if they find anybody, I hope it's firemen with kids, because that's what Patty would have wanted, and Patty would have wanted *you* to want that. I wish everyone could have come out, but you didn't want him to be the sole survivor. If you really love Patty, and you knew him, it's not what he would have wanted.

SEANE CORN

When 9/11 happened, when the buildings went down, aside from my brother, who worked down there, Pat was the first person I thought about. And I knew he died. I was devastated, but I wasn't sad. No doubt in my mind—as everyone was running down, Pat was running up. And I knew that if he was gonna die anywhere, there was no other place. So, I definitely grieved him. I also have a lot of gratitude, because I think he was already a yogi in the making when I knew him earlier. And it was so exciting to know that he took that truth, *his* truth, and that he kept evolving, and that he did touch so many people.

PETE BONDY – FDNY Rescue 2, Retired
CHARLIE WILLIAMS – Battalion Chief, FDNY

PB: It's funny how you think about different people you know, that when you started getting lists of people who died in 9/11, and it's a strange thing, and maybe you'll misunderstand me, but I think Pat *had* to die in 9/11. It would have been unacceptable for him not to die in 9/11.

   CW: I'm sure he felt there was a mission to be accomplished, and he was gonna go try to accomplish it.

   PB: …and he'd be the first one, as high as he could possibly go, and I think in a lot of cases, probably in eighty percent of the cases, guys who tried the hardest to get to the top were the ones who were lost. I think it's almost impossible to be there in that time period, and be alive. A few exceptions. And Pat had to. And anybody that says that the buildings could come down is a liar. Never in a billion years. They never have—there've been numerous high-rise fires, and they've never fallen down. No matter how horrendous the fire.

CW: If they didn't come down when the plane hit 'em, there was no reason to think they were gonna come down.

PB: And even if you thought they might, that is all negative thinking. That's the impressive thing about the fire department—they're hardwired to do the opposite.

CW: You couldn't have accepted or even fathomed a story or a picture of the firefighters running away, and not running into the building.

GEORGE MENAR

If he knew the buildin' was gonna fall, he still woulda went in, 'cause that's the way he was. Try to save, do what he can.

JUDITH SIMON PRAGER

"A Hero For Our Time" (excerpt from *Chicken Soup for the Soul of America,* 2002)

In the days before September 11, 2001, America was a little short on role models. Oh, we had basketball players, rock stars, and millionaires, but there was a dearth of larger-than-life, genuine heroes. In those carefree, careless days, we had no one to show us how to *be*: how to be brave, how to be kind, how to be generous, how to be valiant.

Soldiers had come home from Vietnam, not war heroes but burned out and angry, and among them was one—bedecked in medals—whose inner need for an outlet for the fury inside found its expression in the blaze of firefighting. I remember the first time I met Lieutenant Patrick Brown. It was in 1991, and by then he had become one of the most decorated firefighters in New York City. It was over dinner with a mutual friend in a restaurant where the staff knew and respected him. I was enchanted by his easy charm, the contrast between his ordinary-guy demeanor and his perceptive philosophy. And then, within days, I turned on CNN to see Patrick and another firefighter lying on their bellies on the roof of a building holding a one-inch rope in their bare hands, anchored to nothing, as another firefighter swung on the rope and rescued first one and then another frightened man from the window of a burning building. "The guy was going to jump if we didn't act right away, and there wasn't anything to tie the rope to," Patrick explained, his hands abraded to shreds.

In 1999, *Time* magazine did a cover story on "Why We Take Risks" and featured Captain Patrick Brown among the extreme skiers and race-car drivers. It was an odd juxtaposition from the start. Patrick's picture was a bit formal, but his quote was typical Pat. He said that in the FDNY you were trained not to take "stupid risks." It was never about money or thrills, he said, only for "the greater good." When the article came out, he sent me a copy with a note that showed he was a little mystified at the honor…and the company.

As his legend grew, so did his spirit. He was relentless in his efforts to save those in need. It was said that if there were children or animals trapped in a burning building, Patrick was the one to send in. He had a special radar for the weakest among us, as if his heart were a magnet. The other firefighters admired, even loved him and called him "Paddy." The women loved him—he was so handsome. I thought he looked like a young Clark Gable—and we called him Patrick.

The more intensely he desired to help others, the more expansively he grew inside. He began to study yoga, saying it helped him find "the beauty of life again." He even tried, to no avail, to get the other firefighters to practice with him. In an article in *USA Today*, his yoga teacher, Faith Fennessey, called him "an enlightened being."

He trained for and received a black belt in karate, and then turned around and taught self-defense to the blind. He became incandescent, and yet if you had said so to his face, he would have shaken his head and changed the subject.

In 2001, I was writing a book with my partner, Judith Acosta, about words to say when every moment counts—words that can mean the difference between panic and calm, pain and comfort, life and death. And when I thought of life and death, I thought of Patrick. So I gave him a call. "What do you do, what do you say," I asked, "when you encounter someone who's badly burned, maybe dying?"He became thoughtful, almost shy, as he said that when things are at that terrifying pitch and lives are on the line, he tries to "spend a moment with the victim in silent meditation. Sometimes for just a few seconds, sometimes longer. It depends on the situation," he said. "With some victims, I will put my hands on them and do a little meditation, breathe into it, think into the universe and into God. I try to connect with their spiritual natures, even if they're dying. It helps to keep me calm as much as I hope it helps them."

On September 11, Patrick Brown arrived at the World Trade Center, focused with a clarity of vision that bore through smoke and flames. It is said that someone yelled to him, "Don't go in there, Paddy!" and it was reported that he answered, "Are you nuts? We've got a job to do!" I knew him better. Those weren't his words. So I was relieved when I talked to the men at Ladder 6 and they told a different story. One of the firefighters told me, "When they shouted to him not to go in, he said, 'There are *people* in there.'" Of course.

Another firefighter, who also spoke of how much they all admired Patrick, said, "I saw him enter the lobby and his eyes were *huge*. You know how he gets."Yes. Drawn to battle. Drawn to serve. X-ray vision at the ready.

I visited Ladder 3, his company that had been devastated by the loss of twelve of their twenty-five brothers, and asked about Patrick. Lieutenant Steve Browne told me that, before he met Patrick, he had been a little worried about the new captain because he was such a legend. Surely he could be full of himself and difficult. And then Patrick walked in. "And he was just so…modest," Browne said. "He was just too good to be true. He always stood up for his men, no matter who he had to stand up to. You can't teach what he knew." Another firefighter said of him, "He touched a lot of lives."

I knew that as a friend he had never gotten over the deaths of some of his men in Vietnam. The medals never helped him sleep one bit better. By the time we met, he had also lost men on the job, and each loss tore at him like the eagle that tore out the liver of Prometheus (who, it happens, was punished for stealing fire from the gods to give to mankind.) When Patrick went into the World Trade Center that fateful day, those who knew him agreed that he could not have lived through the grief of losing men one more time. If his men had died, and he had not, we believed, he would never have recovered.

And so, as we waited to hear the names of those lost in the tragedy, we hardly knew how to feel. A week later, the friend who had introduced us, finally, against her own better judgment and wracked with fears, walked over to the firehouse to learn his fate. There sat Patrick's car, where he had left it before the disaster. It hadn't been moved. There was no one to move it. She turned away and went home. Hesitating again, she dialed his number. The phone rang and the message—in his wonderful, gravelly Queens-accented voice—answered and, she told me, "I knew I was hearing a dead man." And we both cried.

These days, since September 11, people have come to recognize that heroes aren't necessarily the richest, most popular people on the block—they are the most valiant, selfless people among us. A

Halloween cover of the *New Yorker* magazine featured children dressed up as firefighters and police officers.

America has a new kind of role model now, one who has shown us how to *be*. After the evacuation order, as others were leaving the building, someone heard Patrick call out over the radio, "There's a working elevator on 44!" which means he had gotten that far up and was still and forever rescuing. And then the apocalyptic whoosh.

I know it must be true that if you died with Patrick by your side, you died at peace. That was his mission. He was where he had to be, where he was needed, eyes wide, heart like a lamp, leading the way to heaven.

*"A broken heart is a whole heart. A leaning ladder is a straight
ladder."*
— Rabbi Menachem Mendel

Independence Day. A day I will always associate with Pat.

Journal Entry – July 5, 1997
Summer continues. A year ago today, I woke up with Pat for the last time.
We had a very cuddly, intimate sleep, and a pleasant morning over coffee
and papers. Most of all, I remember at the elevator he gave me a spontaneous hug and called me one of his pet phrases, "Good girl." Was it a con-
scious last response to all that was loving and comfortable and familiar in
me, in an open and positive way? Because from then on, he shut me out.
He just had to catch himself, and push me away. And so he did. I still get
sad, thinking about it.

Journal Entry – July 4, 2004
The two years after he had broken off our relationship in 1996 were a
time of grief and confusion, my efforts to communicate with any hope
dashed to bits against the despairing shores of his mind. I did not know yet
that Pat's PTSD was such a powerful undertow in his struggle to find happiness and accept love. A turbulent ebb and flow of pulling me in and
pushing me away had settled, finally, into a murky and dark swamp by that
summer of '98. Then I got the phone call.

Journal Entry – July 5, 1998

I got home at 5:30 to one message on the machine. "Hey, Sharon, it's Pat Brown." The last name included: an awkward formality that was perplexing yet somehow understandable. Still it took two playings to sink in that he was inviting me to see the fireworks with him from his apartment that evening. I was so taken aback, I had to sit down and think. All the while, never a doubt in my mind that I would go. Surprisingly, not too nervous, still probably numb, I found my way through the maze of pathways in Stuyvesant Town to his doorstep. I hadn't been with him in that apartment since July 4, 1996—two years to the day.

Journal Entry – July 3, 2004

In the hot, humid holiday weekend of 1999, after yet another year's hiatus, again we connected. And again, fireworks. We shyly joked about a "Same Time Next Year" routine but instead resumed a relationship that lasted through the new millennium, filled with physical intensity and emotional tentativeness. It was different, the second time around. Gone were the euphoric highs. Gone, too, it seemed, were the dark and frightening lows. I took solace in what we now had—a maturation of trust and friendship, a history with each other, and still, the comfort of the carnal. But, of course, this wasn't Paradise. And there was trouble in it.

And so, on this weekend four years after the last time I experienced both Macy's and Pat's fireworks, I am celebrating a small act of personal independence. Yesterday, I went on a sort-of first date with a local man whom I like. He is a "townie," who in my eyes is unusual and intriguing for his proclivity toward quiet adventures in nature, taking joy in what is right outside his door as well as what is half-a-globe away. He's not a gung-ho extreme-sport pursuer, but a modest man who in his world does amazing things. Sound familiar? We hiked to the top of Mt. Beacon, he nursing a hangover from an impromptu rendezvous with old friends the night before, and me nursing one from a rendezvous with ghosts of Pat.

Journal Entry – July 16, 2004

The longer I live outside the city, the weaker its pull on me, or is it my grasp that is letting go? I travel in today on a much delayed business errand, rolled back on a wave of inertia that has drawn me out to sea. My illustration career is the sediment swirling around my ankles, kicked up a little from time to time, but by and large lying stagnant at the bottom of my life. And instead of being able to pour myself full-force into calling people who knew Pat, following leads, preparing for a book-proposal submission before Mercury goes into retrograde (not a good time for communication), I feel trapped in an aspic of free-floating anxiety, simultaneously agitated and paralyzed.

I drift toward the East Village, now a pretty vest-pocket theme park replicating the old, hip, slightly dangerous and charismatic New York of the 1980s. Initially in search of a classic Greek diner for a tuna on rye, I settle for an overpriced veggie burger, sit at an outdoor café, and watch the parade on St. Mark's Place. There they all are——the twenty-somethings with their ubiquitous cell phones and laptops and screenplays and headshots. Pondering them through sunglasses with lenses polarized with deja-vu, I wonder, Was I ever truly ambitious? Passionate, yes. Energized, certainly. I was plugged into that urban battery charger full-time, from the moment I arrived in September 1971, 'til the early 90s. Then I noticed my passions getting murkier, harder to define. The ones that didn't become extinct spun themselves into cocoons of mystery. And now slowly they emerge, entirely new creatures—beautiful but in need of some wing stretching, still not quite able to soar. And the ones that do take off…where are they heading?

Why do I still walk to the intersection of 12th Street and Second Avenue as if drawn by a magnet? Am I indulging a bittersweet memory or touching a bruise, making sure I still feel it? I tentatively approach the corner with the movie theatre that shows slightly off-beat fare. Standing there where I stood then, under the marquee that for months on end spelled out David Lynch's *The Straight Story,* as I waited for Pat to get off work at

Ladder 3. Even if he were coming from somewhere else, we met on that corner. I would inevitably get there first, plant myself in the cold, and peer in all directions. Then I would see him across the street in a holding pattern of a jog, waiting for the light—magnificent cheekbones flushed and a street-vendor knit ski hat pulled down to those black Irish brows, bracketing electric blue eyes that never missed a thing, always searching and anticipating what might happen. As he approached, he would lighten up and assume a playful karate stance while greeting me: "Hey, Wattsky!"

Journal Entry – July 21, 2004

A dog day afternoon in Union Square Park; the sweat under my crossed legs slides my thigh askew, and the weight of my journal adds to the momentum. Right now, it feels like dead weight—a stillborn baby.

The day began on a euphoric high as I dropped off my proposal and manuscript excerpt for *Miss You, Pat* with the mailroom of a major publishing house. The label was addressed to a man considered to be royalty among publishing editors. And not unsolicited, I might add. I was given an excited green light by a contributor to my collection, who knows him personally and who has been published herself with his house. A shot in the dark—I wasn't kidding myself it wasn't, but still! Incredible good fortune to have that shot, to take that aim.

Next on the day's agenda was a meeting with a published author, who gave me his ear and then presented me with very practical and very sobering advice. Which was basically, if my book can't be described in two sentences and be marketed in order to sell, I could forget about my vision, as I know it. Then, the most painful nugget to digest (which I suppose came as no surprise)—that the 9/11 "marketing moment" is over. Painful not that it is over, but that it ever was categorized in marketing terms to begin with. Yet, I am not that naïve, am I? Wasn't I bucking that trend from the get-go? Trying to dig deeper into the meaning of memory, trying to use love and effort and perseverance as healing tools to keep Pat alive for the people who miss him, and for future generations to look back at how such a person lived and died—spectacularly off the Richter scale of human endeavor. Is any of that marketable? Can Matt Lauer pitch that?

Journal Entry – July 29, 2004

Antonio Salieri was the Baroque composer who came to realize (at least, according to the 1984 film *Amadeus*) that he had led a creative life hovering closer to mediocrity than genius. It took Mozart, that impudent wunderkind, to show him the truth, which ate at Salieri until the end of his years.

I have no such point of reference to torture me. Instead, I feel as if I swim in a cultural pool of mediocrity at best, with its surface currents and no depths. The visuals of this world are tired rehashes of kitsch and comfort from all the previous decades of my life; the audio is warmed-over irony, left on the burner too long. It is a world whose shelf life is commensurate with our collective cultural Attention Deficit Disorder. I know there are beacons in the dark that can guide, but they are few and far between. I try and infuse my writing with something that might even dimly reflect the eloquence of Beryl Markham, but feel like a little girl playing dress-up. I feel like Salieri, but without the bile. And I realize I am not a wunderkind of any kind.

Journal Entry – August 13, 2004

Yesterday, I happily spent eight hours in the company of an avid cigar-smoker. Retired Rescue 2 "superman" firefighter Pete Bondy welcomed me to his home on Long Beach, a far cry from the ghettoes of Brooklyn where he spent twenty years contributing to the legendary status of that elite rescue company.

I knew all along that accessing Rescue 2 would not be easy. They were tough as their bulldog mascot—obsessively aggressive, aggressively obsessive—and I imagined they would chew me up and spit me out before I could say, "I'm collecting stories about Pat Brown." And I knew none of them.

By the time I met Pat, he had already evolved into the distinguished and well-respected Captain of Engine 69, The Harlem Hilton. His Rescue 2 years were a decade earlier—"the cowboy years," when his adrenaline pumped as wild and steady as the fire hoses in that crazily busy borough. His skills and senses were all being honed into the razor-sharp acumen that would make him the officer he was to become, and his legendary status was being forged into the annals of the FDNY with the rescues. The medals began crowding his chest, and on the annual Medal Day, he practically wore a path up to the podium at City Hall. Yet Pat would have been the first to point out that rescue is a group effort. That the medals were for all the men, or maybe more for the public and families. His reward was the save itself; the medal was a reminder. And it was his Brooklyn Citizen's Medal that meant the most to him. I know, because he gave it to me that Christmas of 1995.

He told me that he left Rescue 1 to join Rescue 2. The simple reason—more action. For anyone who really knew Pat, it made perfect sense.

CHARLIE WILLIAMS
PETE BONDY

CW: Patty came and just wanted to go to work.

PB: My memory of Patty Brown, at the time, was Charles Bronson. He was a Charles Bronson character. I mean, he was much younger than Charles Bronson, but that "look," and the quiet, and when he talked, everybody listened. 'Cause he rarely spoke. And he was right on target when he did speak. But he was mostly a listener. And he was always there.

CW: We'd go to fires; I loved working alongside him, because he had great instincts. He really did.

PB: He was there at Rescue 2 so much, he'd show up at fires when he wasn't working. He was always involved with things; he'd show up at fires at 4:00 a.m. You get the impression that the firehouse was his whole life, and then years later, you hear different stories and you meet different people and you hear the other aspects of his life and it's like, Wow! Wow! Wow! We thought every aspect of his life was in Rescue 2, but we were one compartment of his life and never really understood all the other things Pat did because he didn't mix them. Like there's forty-seven different avenues, and you thought he's just a firehouse hermit.

CW: He never talked about anything personal. He would never sit down and start telling stories.

PB: We eventually found out he had a dramatic military career; he never talked about it. Then he had these places he went to, and never talked about that. And these other aspects. Like, you get a little seed of it but never the whole thing, and then you realize—there's stuff *every*where! He did everything and went everywhere.

CW: I remember hearing about something with blind people. It didn't surprise me he'd do that, but, we didn't *know* it.

PB: It got to a point where you could go to Cleveland and mention his name in the airport—

CW: —And somebody would know him...

PB: "Oh! I know him, too!" And two different people...I mean, everybody had this tremendously high regard for him, and it had nothing to do with the other part... "Oh, he was in the fire department? Rescue 2?" You know, that kind of stuff. He was all there, one hundred percent, wherever he went. So, it was like putting a puzzle together. I think he did everything one hundred percent, and I don't think he was ever grasping and looking for different things; I think he was just very interested. He had a lot of capacity to learn different things, a lot of curiosity.

CW: There was just stuff we didn't know, 'cause he never talked about it, and meanwhile, that's what I find strange—that he could be like that, yet you still considered him your friend. I mean, I loved him, and I always knew he loved me. One of the last fires I saw him at was on the East Side, at Waterside Tower in April, 2001, and I just finished walkin' up the stairs 'cause I didn't get there 'til the fire was almost out, and I'm on the floor below the fire, and who do I see comin' down? And he's beat, he's beat up good, and he's checkin' his guys and he sees me, and I go, "Patty, you okay?" And he goes, "Charlie! That was some hot fire!" It was just great to see him. Just great to see him.

BRENDA BERKMAN – Captain, Engine 239, FDNY
I can't even remember when I first met Pat. He was sort of ubiquitous; everybody knew who he was. And people knew who I was, not as a person, but as the woman who got the first FDNY women firefighters hired. Of course, that didn't win me any popularity contests, especially in the beginning. And so, for any male firefighter to be friendly or even courteous to me, let alone show any interest in my career or help me in any way—that was an anomaly. And that was how Pat stood out.

Fairly early on, he'd talk to me at times when all the other male firefighters were shunning me. And it didn't seem to bother him at all. I always got the impression that he was interested in change in the fire department. And that women coming on were a part of that, and he didn't view it necessarily as a negative thing.

I think in some ways he felt himself a bit of an outcast—not a "company man." And yet he was very highly respected for his skills and his heroism. But he wasn't "chesty" about it. Some guys think that because they're in Rescue or in a certain house, they're inherently superior. But I never got that from Pat.

He was a little bit of an oddball. Not very many firefighters live in Manhattan, number one, and it was clear he had wider interests than the fire department. I mean, nobody did yoga! He was his own person—he didn't seem to care that much what other people thought of him.

The last time I saw Pat was the summer of 2001. The two of us were the only off-duty white people to attend the memorial service for Robert Lowery, the first African-American NYC Fire Commissioner. Commissioner Lowery was probably unknown to a huge percentage of people on the job when he died. It impressed me a lot that Pat was there.

Most white people cannot identify with oppression, period. But even if they have some experience with it, whether it's sexual orientation or ethnicity or gender or disability, they tend to focus on their own form of oppression. They can't identify with other oppressed groups. It seemed to me that the commonality we all have as human beings was more important to Pat than any differences between us.

Journal Entry – September 28, 2005
I decide to walk across the Brooklyn Bridge starting on the Brooklyn side, take in the Crayola blue sky, the "happy little clouds" dabbed across the shimmering skyline as it now is. As unreal to me as the mass-produced, made-in-China 3-D souvenir art lining 14th Street.

Equally strange—glimpsing what is now gone in a *Seinfeld* rerun, or a movie shot in Soho when Soho was hot. The flutter and flight of trendy clubs gave the Towers validity, a weight, a sense that they always were and always would be authority figures, "cool parents" chaperoning downtown life.

PAT BROWN – *Men's Journal* – April 1998
In Brooklyn, there was a fire on the second floor of a crack house; the third floor was full of regular people. It was crazy, people hanging out of the window. We put an aerial ladder up and into the fire, and they were screaming. I couldn't even see if the ladder was in a window; I just assumed it was. And I was scared shitless, but I kept going up to the fire and I kept burning and I kept coming back. I just kept saying, 'I can't fucking do this,' and then I just ran up through the smoke and heat—thank God it was the window— and I just crashed right through."

Medal Day **Magazine** – June 8, 1988
Patrick Brown is an intense man who is drawn to action. In 1969 he enlisted in the Marine Corps and saw extensive combat duty in the jungles of Vietnam as a sergeant in the Marine Infantry. Upon dis-

charge, Patty was reinstated in the New York City Fire Patrol, serving with distinction until his appointment to the FDNY in 1977. In ten years Patty has become one of the most decorated firefighters in the Department. Holding 20 individual meritorious citations, he is being decorated with his fourth and fifth Medals of Valor today.

On May 26, 1987, at 21 minutes past midnight, Box 693 was transmitted. The second floor of 251 Hart Street, Brooklyn, had been used to process the drug "crack" and contained highly flammable and explosive chemicals, which fed the intense fire conditions as Rescue 2 arrived. Firefighter Pat Brown was informed of trapped occupants on the third floor. He immediately ascended Ladder 102's aerial, which was placed at the third-floor window directly above the heavy heat and smoke venting from the second floor.

As Pat approached the tip of the ladder, fire blew out the windows below, burning his neck and throat. Recovering, he made another effort to enter the window but was driven back by the punishing inferno. Mustering his strength and courage, he raced up the ladder and dove into the flat. The heat was blistering and the smoke so dense that he was forced to crawl. He searched with his hands until he found an unconscious child, Joshua Moll, age 2. Pat grabbed the child and followed the voice of Firefighter Peter Hassler of Ladder 102, who was positioned at the tip of the aerial. He handed the child over to Hassler and reentered the flat to continue his search.

Conditions were deteriorating as the fire extended up the interior public stairs into the apartment that Pat was searching. Undaunted, he found another unconscious child, Joel Moll, age 5. He quickly removed him to the other window where Ladder 111 had placed its bucket. For the third time Pat entered the now blazing flat. Deep inside, he located yet another unconscious victim, Cathlina Moll, age 35, the children's mother. Pat, near total exhaustion, had difficulty removing this victim and called for assistance.

Firefighter Joseph Borst entered the flat in answer to Pat's call. Together they were able to drag the victim to the tower ladder bucket.

Feeling anxious and concerned about the condition of the victims, Pat now accompanied them to the hospital. En route in the EMS ambulance, one victim stopped breathing. Quickly Pat administered mouth-to-mouth resuscitation until the victim was breathing on his own. Thanks to his attentive lifesaving actions, this nearly destroyed family recovered in the hospital.

Pat Brown operated above an extending fire without the benefit of a hose line. He disregarded his own personal safety and at extreme personal risk saved three lives. For his great fortitude and perseverance, the Fire Department of New York is proud to present the Brooklyn Citizen's Medal to Lieutenant Patrick J. Brown.

CHRISTMAS, 1995

Dear Sharon,

You saved me in my old life, and have given me a new life. There are many, many things that I could say about you and your strength and beauty, but this time I want to say something else. There are many things I've learned since we have been together. Here are two.

When I gave you my freedom, I realized what real freedom means. Your (sic) never really free until you give it to someone else.

When I gave you my love, I realized how deep love can be. Only when it is given to someone who deserves it and appreciates it can it be true.

This medal was awarded to me after a horrible fire where we managed to save three kids and the mom. Everybody lived! It was probably my greatest achievement in the Fire Dept. This is the department's second highest medal and it means everything to me. Now I give it to you with all my love. And now it becomes ours.

I love you!! Pat

Journal Entry

"He trusts me because he knows I love his mom."

The innocent sweetness of the words stopped me in the middle of making my bed. Pat had bonded with my cat Rufus, just a few short weeks into our relationship. We were spending more time at my pre-war apartment than Pat's one-bedroom in Stuyvesant Town. And I had three cats for Pat to win over as well as me.

Rufus had been a stray kitten from a lineage of "purebred" Brooklyn alley cats born over and over again in the courtyard behind 201 Eastern Parkway. He grew up in the basement of my building, living in the pipes and somehow evading a violent eviction. Three years before Pat and I met, I took Rufus into my life, and (after seven flea baths) gave him love, food, warmth, and safety. But he still hid in my closet whenever anyone visited. Anyone, that is, except Pat.

Pat was very specific in his surmising of Rufus's traumatic history. He suspected that Rufus had been a victim of attempted garroting, because Rufus never allowed any two hands on him at any one time. I look back and ponder Pat's own childhood trauma, which led to his bonding with an orphaned and abused cat. How safe did he ever feel? In places that any child should feel safe—at home, in school or church, and later, serving his country cloaked in the belief of its ideals—Pat experienced the worst that adults can impart on a boy, and learned that trust was a hard concept to embrace. And yet the child in him persisted to search, and sometimes find.

When he shared his personal history with me, it was simply dropped into our conversation. No cue cards or coaching for my reaction. I absorbed what he said without prying, and tried to let him know he was safe with me.

As our relationship progressed, the waters where we floated in perfect equilibrium somehow got turbulent. Did I inadvertently challenge his role as rescuer? Or were we possibly reversing the roles, and struggling with the fit?

Journal Entry – October 28, 2005

The Metropolitan Improvement Company is hard to find, tucked in a section of lower Manhattan not on any tourist map. Behind the fortress of One Police Plaza and butting up against Chinatown public housing, the four-or-so-block area is crosshatched with dotted lines of streets predating the Civil War. They have names like Oliver Street, St. James, Dover—real trivia challenges. The "Met" is on Madison. Street, not Avenue.

I am early for my meeting with a cousin of Pat's, once or twice removed, and his wife, in from San Diego. Jim, who has only dim and sparse memories of Pat from visiting the Brown family in Queens Village as a young boy, is fascinated by how Pat's life evolved. The focus of one memory is sharp, however. The older cousins, Pat and Mike, fling potatoes at each other in the kitchen while the grownups sling back cocktails in the living room.

The "Happy Hour" drink this Friday is the martini. I opt for merlot and take in the surroundings. It's an old-fashioned pub, with a TV pitched loudly, an Irish barmaid, and off-duty cops perched on the stools. The "Met" is owned by the tall and genteel Don Brown, Jr., a cousin of Pat's father, John. Pat came from a family in law enforcement, and for years there was only one acknowledgement to the FDNY on the walls—the news photo of Pat in the roof rope rescue. Now there is an entire wall of Pat. As a baby-faced Marine. In action with Rescue 2. Smiling with Mayor Dinkins after the brouhaha. And standing next to his beaming father.

Pat was always embraced and celebrated by his family in this small restaurant/pub after the Medal Day awards at nearby City Hall. Here his father could show his pride in his firstborn son—something that probably wasn't easily done in Irish-Catholic families of a certain generation, in the intimacy of a family kitchen, or living room.

JIM ACHENBACH

The relationship between Pat Brown and myself is blood; my dad was Pat's mom's cousin. I often saw Mr. John Brown, Pat's dad, at my house.

Although the two were both FBI agents, the relationship was based on friendship rather than employment or family ties.

In a very strange way, I did grow up with Pat Brown. My father was a Marine, Pat's dad was a Marine, Pat a Marine. I was reminded of this on a regular basis, growing up with stories of my father's experience with a conclusion of, "Your cousin is a hero from the Vietnam War."

I was living in the Bronx, away at college, when my mother called to tell me what Pat had done. He had invited Mayor Dinkins to his firehouse to discuss the needs of his firemen. Our conversation strolled down the road, my mother and I wondering where Pat would end up since he had extended his invitation on television. All of this, added to my mother's understanding of New York politics. Strange, I recall this conversation like it was yesterday, and never did the fact surface that the reason for Pat's TV interview was a heroic rescue. Classic Pat.

I was in New York the last week of August 2001, near 13th Street. I wanted to stop and introduce myself, but felt foolish. Now I feel sad that I did not take the time. I went to Pat's funeral on the 9th of November, his birthday, and learned what a great man he was.

I can tell you that I have changed more after 11/9 than 9/11. I know it is not about me, and when I catch myself, I stop and ask Pat to give me the strength to do the right thing, to enter my own burning building to assist the strangers who cross my life.

RICHARD ENGEL – Pat's Childhood Friend
Undoubtedly, many people will say that Pat Brown left a mark on their lives. But I can say that in the literal sense. Every morning when I wake up and look in the mirror, I think about Pat. The first thing I see is the prominent scar in the middle of my forehead, a result of falling into a cast-iron radiator at Pat's house and splitting my head open while clowning around. The scar was covered by my hair through my early twenties, but once my hairline receded, it became very noticeable. Although it is not a pretty sight, the scar is something I am proud of.

I was a friend and classmate of Patrick Brown's, growing up in Queens Village. Our neighborhood was sandwiched between the Long Island Railroad, Cross Island Parkway and Hempstead Avenue. The residences in the area were a mix of single-family homes, two- and three-story row houses, and apartment buildings, occupied primarily by hard-working, blue-collar families. Across from the railroad tracks were industrial buildings, including a bread factory, Wise Potato Chips, Howard Johnson's food distribution, and the local fire house. Queens Village had both a bus and train station, so getting to NYC and Long Island by public transportation was fairly easy.

The neighborhood was very active, and with the concentration of homes and families, there were always a lot of kids around. It was easy to get a team together to play baseball, football, or basketball, or else we would play stickball or just ride our bikes.

Pat's mom Ruth was a piano teacher and taught lessons in her home, so we usually had to be pretty quiet when we were there. After Pat's sister Carolyn was born, Mrs. Brown kept her at her feet during the piano lessons. I remember Carolyn with her light wispy hair and big, bright eyes taking everything in. It was clear that Mrs. Brown was thrilled to have a little baby girl in the house. Mrs. Brown was a very kind and gentle woman, and we always felt comfortable around her.

Mr. Brown was in the FBI and worked a lot of hours. He was a tall man with a quiet but imposing presence. Pat's dad was also a good baseball player and made it onto the NY Yankees farm team. He was a teammate and friend of Yankee stars Whitey Ford and Yogi Berra. Mr. Brown coached Little League baseball for several years, and my dad was his assistant coach.

On the first day of summer, all of the kids in our group would meet at the barber shop and get crew cuts. Pat and his brother Mike both had big round heads that looked even bigger after the crew cuts. Pat looked like a fuzzy peach and Mike looked like a round Duncan Yo-Yo, so we called them Peach and Yo-Yo. My nickname was Turtle, probably because I didn't run very fast.

A few of us used to spend a lot of time at the Brown's, playing with Pepe the dog, taking care of homing pigeons, and just being kids. The Brown house was a large colonial with a detached garage. Not every house had a garage, and since many families were lucky to even have one car, the garages had alternate uses, like storage, a workshop, or a clubhouse. Pat Brown's garage, however, got heavy use as a fire training structure.

Located just a few blocks away from all of our homes, the local fire house, Engine 304, became a local meeting spot. When we weren't playing baseball, we would ride our bikes to the firehouse. There we'd help the firemen clean the trucks, organize equipment, and do other errands. It was especially exciting if a fire call came in when we were at the house because we'd learn where the alarm was located and go racing off on our bikes to the emergency.

When we got back from a call, we would watch the fire squad park the trucks and unload their gear. Then head back to the Brown's garage and practice what we just saw the firemen do on their call, using a wooden ladder, hoses, and gear—all stored behind the garage.

In the fifth and sixth grades, Pat took more of an interest in the FDNY than the rest of us. He got a police scanner and was able to hear the fire and police emergencies live, over the air. He started going to fires outside the neighborhood, branching out to the rest of Queens, and then to the other boroughs, especially the Bronx and Manhattan, where there was a lot more action. By the seventh grade Pat knew the entire NYC Transit System by heart, and he typically showed up to school smelling like smoke after being at a fire all night. Pat was the ultimate fire buff, so we gave him the name of Buff Chief. It was clear that this was his calling and that he would stand out head and shoulders above everyone else.

Like the rest of the gang, we went our separate ways after grade school. Our families moved from the neighborhood, so it was hard to keep in touch. I took the fire department exam with Pat in high school and had aspirations to get in, but it didn't work out. I know my life would have been much different if I entered the FDNY. However, I don't think I would have come even close to making the contributions that Pat made to the department. I was always impressed when I read about his exploits, and always felt lucky to be associated with him. And sad that he is no longer with us.

"Work out your own salvation. Do not depend on others."——BUDDHA

Journal Entry – August 22, 2004

When I rewind my answering machine all the way, it goes back to September 4, 2001, to a message I have never erased, certainly not on purpose and so far not even accidentally. That last phone call from Pat was made the night of the day that became the very last time I saw him. Two blocks from the Ladder 3 fire house, and he was heading toward me in a half-jog, on his way to yoga class, upbeat and smiling. I was happy to see him so happy; by some accounts, he had been having a tough summer. He and I had become estranged after my move upstate, and Pat, a man who needed the rituals and semblances of routine, had to assimilate my physical move out of his life, or at least out of his city. Of greater weight, there were more friends' deaths with the Father's Day fire in Queens, and then later in August came the emotional strain of taking care of his father on Long Island after his hip-replacement surgery. Ghosts of demons from childhood must have hovered as he took care of the tough FBI dad who had not always taken care of him. A close friend of Pat's was visiting from California, and together they frequented AA meetings and yoga classes, different paths to healing but each coming with the price of some honest pain.

The phone message, when I rewind, starts: "Hey, Sharon, it's Pat." His slightly tired, gravelly voice catches my heart with a gentle snag. Then the next message, saved just a few months this summer with a different voice, lighter, not so familiar yet, is my first phone call from Michael. The "townie." Michael is a miracle. Without his even knowing it, he has begun to restore me with the care that he would use on an old cane chair. He is the only person who makes me feel completely alive, hopeful, renewed. I hear the two messages back-to-back and reflect on my own price paid, a price I thought I could never afford.

Journal Entry – September 1, 2004

I have to acknowledge the dark veil of memory that settles over me, as if turning the calendar page from August to September releases it automatically, almost imperceptibly, to envelope me until the anniversary of 9/11 has passed.

Michael left earlier this week for Colorado. It frees me up to be alone with my feelings and thoughts, while I am caught in the dark veil. Caught, but not struggling. At this time, I simply resign myself to "be." But I think of Michael, and I think of Pat. I try not to balance the two, not wanting to presume one should outweigh the other. That's not a law of physics that exists in my world.

Journal Entry – September 11, 2004

It is now three years to the day that I was aware of Pat's fate, in my gut and heart. I sit on the same city-bound train, staring through dirty windows at the sky. The same perfect promise of a blue heaven makes me want to etch my thoughts into the grimy film on the glass. Then I want to get out the Windex and clear it all away. I sit on a seat that faces backward. I want to look at my life facing forward, to be in the driver's seat, and I want clean, clear windows. I want a rear-view mirror that never fogs; and fuzzy dice that come up lucky sevens more often than not. I want to leave the repair shop, ready for the road again.

Journal Entry – September 11, 2004, *continued*

I thought I would be hyper-aware of the time, 10:28 a.m., when the North Tower fell, while Pat was spending his last moment on this earth guiding and comforting others. I thought I'd be walking through Grand Central Terminal, in a crowd, and look at the big clock, and as the minute hand approached the exact dot—think, feel, acknowledge, pray.

Not 'til almost eleven, as I was headed to Brooklyn on the subway, did I look at my watch. It read 10:50 a.m., and a jolt went through me—I missed it! What had I been doing? Where was my mind at this crucial time I had pre-mapped into my day and then missed?

I rewound and remembered a man was guiding his wife to the entrance of the ladies' restroom at Grand Central. I followed her in and realized she had a cane and was blind. I helped her navigate the terrain, and led her out to her husband and son, who were waiting with anxious and then relieved expressions. A nice, suburban-looking family that thanked me profusely for such a small act.

We all have to negotiate dark rooms, unknown places, sometimes on our own and sometimes with the help of a stranger. At 10:28 a.m., Pat Brown was helping me help someone else in a small way.

Journal Entry – March 18, 2005

The Pat Project has been dormant for most of this past winter. I didn't intend to lose interest or abandon it, but my labor of love somehow had grown into a haphazard research column of papers and articles and books, mortared together with guilty neglect. Torn slips of paper with potential contact names and scribbled phone numbers would fall to the floor and gather dust, 'til finally I'd shove them back into the pile with a trowel of intent to organize and proceed.

Who knows what finally pushed my brain's chemicals over the edge? All I knew at the time was that I was not me. It was as if a finger had pressed down on a glob of mercury and dispersed an army of small silver pellets skittering around my skull, collecting dirt, and refusing to rejoin and cooperate. Clinical depression. A phrase I had always known in theory, as it related to others. Friends, authors whose memoirs led us down those dark halls, doctors who informed and encouraged us in women's magazines. And Pat.

That Pat was sometimes a sad and troubled man became evident as our wedding plans progressed. Or rather, didn't. Reading through my old journals, I see a gap where things started to unravel. Too confused or exhausted to write or conjecture, too busy learning to walk on the eggshells of the newly hatched elephant in the room. I simply couldn't understand then what I now grasp in hindsight.

Over the years, I've tried to imagine what Pat must have felt. He threw himself into "us" with such force and abandon and hope and trust—defying that wall to stop us. That wall he knew so well. In my own naiveté, and with my own force, abandon, hope, trust, I stood there in front of Pat's wall from the other side and hammered, whacked, chiseled, and chipped—physically and emotionally spent, trying to understand and overcome the enemy.

By early summer of 2001, I was out of the city, living upstate. Pat and I were at an impasse yet again. I had thrown some new parameters and perimeters into our dance of intimacy, yet I had no fear that it was the last dance. There would always be a do-si-do in our future. It simply was in our chemistry, and in our history.

And so, I was setting up my first house, my first garden, driving my first car—a new life. Along with this, almost as if it had woven itself into a cocoon during those difficult years and was now ready to emerge as a butterfly, was an epiphany: Pat woke up every single morning and tried, so hard, to be the best person he possibly could be. That was the essential truth and purity of intent that was Patrick J. Brown. Realizing that truth erased all my previous pain, and I knew I wanted him in my life on whatever terms he was comfortable with. I had finally let go, and with that appeared the elusive holy grail of adult understanding—unconditional love. My enemy was vanquished.

EAPEN CHACKO – Seido Karate Student – 2002

About ten years ago, I assisted at a grading promotion at Seido Karate headquarters in New York. There was a group of students going for their next belt. One of them was a yellow belt student who was older than many of the other students; this man was evidently very strong physically, and very committed. His face was serene but also bore a lot of experience and a tinge of sadness. I carried the distinct memory and image of this man, without a name, for many years.

Last year, I attended a ceremony at Seido headquarters to celebrate their twenty-fifth anniversary, but also to remember one of our own who had perished trying to save others in the collapsing World Trade tower. This man was a highly decorated captain in the fire department, as well as being an honored veteran of the Vietnam conflict. Friends told stories about Pat Brown, especially about his humility and willingness to go the extra mile to help anybody, not just a friend. This was the same man whose face I remembered from the karate promotion many years ago. It was very sad, but also wonderful to know and understand something about such a marvelous person who was always in my memory, but without a name, until then.

JIMMY S. – Officer, NYPD

I met Pat Brown while I was assigned to P.S.A. #6 (Police Service Area, a housing police station house) around the corner from his firehouse, the "Harlem Hilton" (Engine 69/Ladder 28) on 143rd Street and 8th Avenue. We were both students of Kaicho Nakamura, Grandmaster of Seido Karate.

I spent an evening with Pat. We went to an AA meeting and then for sushi at Taste of Tokyo in the Village. Our conversation was about our jobs, recovery, and being sober men and not caricatures of masculinity. I recall talking about the John Wayne syndrome and how "the job" has changed. I had recently left uniformed work in Harlem and was assigned to the faculty at the Police Academy; I was putting together a video and a lesson to be called: "Stress in Police Work: An Inside Job."

My ambition was, while protecting their anonymity, to speak candidly to members of the service about their experiences with alcohol-abuse as well as depression, self-destruction, troubled relationships, financial difficulties, frustration, etc. I wanted the essence of an AA meeting to touch people who might otherwise never experience one. I wanted to offer some hope to anyone who was still suffering. Having heard Pat speak about some of his experiences, it was clear to me that he should be part of this work. Certainly there wasn't *that* much difference between cops and firemen, was there?

Over dinner I asked, "Pat, barring your health and your freedom, if you had to lose everything with one exception, what would that one thing be?" Without hesitation, as if he had all night to prepare for this question, he said softly, "Serenity." I was amazed——Vietnam veteran, Marine Corps infantry sergeant, FDNY captain, dozens of medals, Seido karate black belt, sober alcoholic, gentleman-tough guy... SERENITY?

He drew a large triangle and placed an *S* in the middle and spoke about the Superman complex. Whether it was Superman, John Wayne, Captain Marvel, or whoever, he made the point that the *S* should stand for SERENITY. Confused and realizing his answer was a mile from what I had in mind (and that I was going to have to pick up the check for this dinner), I asked him to tell me what, in his opinion, defined SERENITY.

He wrote on the paper napkin:

SERVICE (done in)
   +

      SILENCE (with no thought of reward or recognition)
     +

        (involving) SACRIFICE (meaning hard work
        against all selfish instincts)
         = SERENITY

"For us," he said, "the *S* we insist on wearing on our chests must stand for SERENITY."

I was impressed and thought, Wow, I can use this. I found it amazing that he could take a concept I would ramble on about, and flatten it into a cogent, succinct, clean phrase that truly spoke the message.

I probably would have forgotten all about this had Pat not been killed on September 11. In consequence, I tell the story to every class I teach. As a result, I memorialize him and keep him in my heart.

DAVID LIFE

It was in Pat's nature to challenge himself in such a way as to make him more available to serving others. Because his motto was: "Other people's lives come before mine." A form of yoga called Karma Yoga has two aspects—you do good works with no expectation of any reward. Which was just like him. And we really emphasize that here—doing the yoga practice from a place of pure intention, with a feeling of service to others. So for Pat, it meshed perfectly with who he already was, how he viewed his contribution to life in general.

I think the yoga practice represented to him a kind of maturation; it's amazing that he could continue to evolve his choices, to embrace more philosophically his whole life view. And that it happened when it did, in his life, was picture-perfect, in a way.

RODNEY HOGAN – Pat's Fellow Yogi Friend

Patrick Brown was a man of Truth; all his life he was trying to find answers that led to Peace. We became friends at Jivamukti Yoga Center. I didn't know who he was. We spoke about life.

He told me what he saw, what it was like in a war, in Vietnam. That you had no idea, unless you were there, what a horrible experience it was. It was too much to handle—it blew his mind. Patrick was a good-hearted person who experienced things in life he never imagined could exist.

He wanted to save lives. He saw enough destruction. But it was a road his heart had to follow, not knowing if, or when, his dream of peace would come through.

At yoga he told me it was the first time he had ever felt happiness and the meaning of love inside himself. Patrick found his other side, the part of his life that was missing. He felt love, contentment, happiness. He told me, "I'll give my life first, to save another." I felt, when I was talking to him, that he was like a saint. I never met such a person, to come out with words like that.

Patrick died the way he wanted to, and in the highest state of yoga— *Samadi*, One with the Self, the Soul. He was in a powerful state of total love, by serving others. Love is the completion of the heart, inside your soul. He reached that.

A prayer takes only one minute a day to say: You went through it all. I know where you are. Bye, it sure was a blessing to have met you. Love always, Rodney.

"What makes men happy is loving to do what they have to do. This is a principle on which society is not founded." ——Helvetius

Journal Entry – March 28, 2005

The Twin Towers are now the ethereal yardsticks for measuring loss within the fire department. In a more innocent time, losing two men, from one horrific back draft, gripped and saddened the city even as a new season unfolded with promise. A third, the captain, kept us all hanging by a thread of hope for forty more days. He couldn't beat the insurmountable odds, not even with his ferociously strong body and fighter's spirit. Nor with his wife's stoic love, coaching him to live, at his bedside in the burn center. Nor with the hopes and prayers of his children, his FDNY family, and, it seemed, the entire city of New York.

Eleven years ago today, the alarm went out for 62 Watts Street, an old walk-up in a nether of Manhattan real estate not yet desirable—not quite Soho, not quite Greenwich Village. The men from my local firehouse of many years, Ladder 5/Engine 24, responded.

I was living in Brooklyn, but it still hit close to home. That was *my* firehouse, no matter where I paid rent. Those were *my* firemen. When I was young, married to Larry, and living a block away, I grew to know their faces and personalities by walking past and exchanging greetings, waves, innocent flirtations. They were always gentlemen. And if I saw a bright blue vintage pickup truck parked in front, it meant my favorite, John, was working. I'd ask the guy on the house watch to call him, sometimes rousing him from a well-earned late-afternoon nap. Still, he'd beam and give me a big bear hug, and we'd sit on the ledge in front while he asked how life was treating me. We shared a love of collecting things from the curb; other people's trash was always a potential treasure. John would show me his latest acquisition, salvaged in the back of his truck, to my delight and I'm sure, his wife's lament. His firehouse compatriots dubbed him "the Junkman," and in his orange Converse and ripped-at-the-knees workpants, and after-hours pierced earring, he could have been a hip neighborhood artist. But he was John, the fireman, who would do anything for anyone. I adored him.

And there was Dennis. A little gruff, very irascible, yet deeply moral within his own code of ethics. It made him enemies, but it also made him loyal friends. John was one of them. When I moved upstate, they immediately agreed to gut and renovate my kitchen. John died on 9/11. Seven months later Dennis started my kitchen and finished the job to the best he was able, as a promise kept more to John than to me. And I understood.

And so, a day or two after the Watts Street fire I headed downtown after a karate class to pay my respects to my firehouse.

The first person I saw, past the mounds of flower arrangements and stuffed animals, was Chris, a tall, lanky walrus of a man, and we hugged. What was there to say? From the back, I heard a voice call out: "Osu, Senpai!" Osu, Senpai? A greeting from a fellow karate-ka, but who? And why, in here, now? Out of the shadows came Pat Brown, a green belt student I recognized from class. His warm smile threw me off guard, and he told me he would be filling in at Ladder 5 while his friend, Captain John Drennan, was holding on.

That summer, I would see Pat at the dojo. We'd exchange shy smiles and greetings, sensing that we would like to say more to each other. Later, I learned a little of what he endured, and what he gave back to the Drennan family during their darkest hour. A small spark between us emerged from the embers of that tragedy.

Washington Post – Sally Jenkins – September 20, 2001

One window of Chumley's is a piece of stained glass glazed with the emblem of the ladder company. An old red call box is bolted to the wall, as is other firehouse memorabilia.

Above the bar, owner Steve Schlopak has hung a framed portrait of a famous department hero, Capt. John Drennan, who perished with two other men in 1994 when he was fighting a fire inside a building and a gas cloud exploded. Drennan was so tough that he lived for 40 days with fourth-degree burns over most of his body.

It was he who best described a firefighter's duty: "Two hundred and twenty days of boredom, and 20 minutes a year of sheer terror."

One of the men missing in the World Trade wreckage is Drennan's best friend, Capt. Pat Brown. "When they find Pat Brown, they'll find him in the densest place, in the highest part of the building, with the most firefighters around him," Schlopak predicted.

VINA DRENNAN – Widow of Captain John Drennan
(Speech given at the Columbians' Holy Name Communion Breakfast where Pat was named Man of the Year, April 23, 1995)

Many of you men have come up to me this past year; you've held my hand and looked into my eyes and asked, "Vina, how are you doing? How are the children?" Women, too, have come up to me this past year. They've held my hand and looked into my eyes and asked, "Vina, what's Patty Brown like?"

People have been kind to me. They have commented on my ability to be strong in dealing with everyone's worst nightmare. Today you honor the person who gave me the courage I needed to cope with this tragedy. I am most grateful that you chose to honor Patrick Brown.

When he entered into my life, I was losing my ability to deal with the enormity of the situation. Those closest to me couldn't deal with the horror of John's injuries—there was no one to lean on. I was exhausted and terrified. I was broken and frightened.

His first words to me were, "I don't talk much, but I've been assigned to you." And he never left, and we never stopped talking. At that point, I was terrified of being left alone, and I didn't know how to beg this man I didn't know not to leave. But he sensed my fear, and he said, "I'll sleep on the couch." And he did—and he took me to a therapist the next day, and he asked Dr. Madden the questions I was too afraid to ask, and he told me what I needed to know. His strength became my strength.

I love Patty Brown. He's the brother I never had and the best friend anyone could ever hope to have. He was there during the glare of the forty days that John struggled to live. He sat alone with John many hours when I couldn't anymore—late into the night he sat, giving comfort by his presence. He talked to John during those quiet, frightening hours and reassured him that the kids were being cared for, that the whole department, indeed, the whole city, was praying for him. We will never know how much that love meant to John and how it might have eased his fears. Who can measure what Patty did for John? But there's nobody that could have done it better—not even me.

And when death came and the suffering ended, he was there. When it was over, when it got lonely, when it got quiet, when it got scary, Patty was there for us still.

Patty did another remarkable thing for me. He let me into his life. When he met his friends, he brought me along. So there I was, an ordinary housewife, a school teacher, with the most good-looking bachelors in New York City, eating in the best restaurants. I used to laugh and say that when the troubles were over, I was going to call Helen Gurley Brown and tell her that I found the best-looking, nicest bachelors in New York. So I thank Patty for sharing his life with me, and I still treasure those friendships very much.

Patrick, I am glad they're honoring you. You are the most noble man I have ever met. I can never repay you for what you have done for me, for John, for my children. In closing, I know when Patty dies and goes to heaven, John Drennan is going to be the first one to welcome him. "Patty," he'll say, "we're both brave, we're both tough, we're both true leaders, heroes who have done great things. But Patty, I was married to Vina for twenty-six years, and there's no way I could have spent forty days in a row with her. Patty, you're the greatest!"

PAT BROWN – NBC, *Dateline* 1994 (interview excerpt)
We (Vina and I) went back in the room for about twenty minutes, just me and her, and cried over his body and stuff. It was kinda beautiful, ya know. If I was faced with the same situation again, I'd do it. As much of a struggle and as tough as it was, it was the greatest honor ever bestowed on me in my life—to be able to not only help John Drennan, but to help care for a man like that's family.

Journal Entry – July 1, 2005
Last week, I received a letter from S., a friend of Pat's, and after 9/11, a friend of mine. In it was an update as to his life. He had recently relapsed and was undergoing rehab in a center situated in a monastery near my house. Also—would I send him Pat's memorial mass card "or anything about Patrick. I miss him."

Graymoor was just twenty-five minutes away. I thought I could drop off the envelope with my homemade "hang in there" card and the requested contents. Maybe if S. was having a good day, he could receive visitors. What did I know about rehab? Not much, except that friends of Pat's and mine need it from time to time.

I myself was having a very bad day. Or week. Or possibly six months. I certainly could have used some twelve-step wisdom. Instead, I put on a favorite summer dress, stopped en route for a gourmet brownie, and approached Graymoor with an air of positive curiosity.

The man at reception looked at me as if I had grown two heads when I inquired about S. Apparently serendipitous social calls were not part of recovery. Neither was leaving an envelope with good wishes, a memorial mass card, and possibly crack cocaine. I must have appeared like a Trojan horse in my vintage pink frock with brownie crumbs dusting my lipstick. I suggested that he open and inspect the envelope while I stood there, but no go. So I skulked out of the building, exasperated more at my own naiveté than the house rules.

I ducked into the thrift shop on the grounds; *any* thrift shop is normally an oasis to me. Still, a feeling that I wasn't in Kansas anymore hung over the veneer furniture, polyester pants, and bad art. "Fifty percent off all frames, excluding religious art." The employees, or volunteers, or penance-doers acknowledged me and went back to their shop talk, which centered around a large grey cat on the countertop.

Wandering about the depressing detritus of those who hopefully went from the twelfth step and into God's loving arms, I was thoroughly bummed out. I had failed to deliver my goodwill packet (which I hoped would be an antidote to my own depressed state). And I had wasted a chunk of a day when I could have been applying myself to my mirage of a career.

As I left, a guy called the cat… "Serenity!" Did I hear right? Like the TV show *Seinfeld*'s famous declaration by George Costanza's father, "I need Serenity, *now!*" But I managed a laugh; every day my own cats give me "Serenity, Meow." And that's a step in the right direction, too.

STEVE BAKER

I didn't ask Pat to be my sponsor, he *told* me. When I relapsed, I thought he should understand, because he had all this time in the AA program. I didn't realize that I hurt him. People who love you—and Patty did love me; he used to call me "Little Stevie"—get hurt. I see that now; I'm learning that now, about other people in my life. I have to go through the darkness and the pain. I'm six months sober, again, and I've learned to discuss my abuse, my shame issues, my PTSD, my grieving.

When you died, Pat, I smoked crack and I didn't want to feel. And then, slowly, I remembered that I want to live. I had to find a new sponsor, and that was hard, but I think that's what you wanted me to do.

When you went through the steps, you felt a very spiritual need to help people, to be a part of life. And that's something you were proud of. You didn't care so much about your anonymity being broken—people respected you for not only what you've done as a fireman, but for who you are as a person. You set a standard of sobriety and recovery.

This is the first I've spoken out about Pat. For us to share him—that's beautiful. If you can't talk about Pat honestly, there's no reason to talk about him at all. He dealt with himself truthfully, and gives us strength to do the same. He inspires us.

What Pat did, he did because it was the *right* thing to do. That was his belief—just do the right thing to help your fellow man. Christianity, Buddhism, any basic philosophy—you always help your fellow man. His life was, in a sense, an open book. And that's what made people come to him, and why I gravitated toward him.

He knew there was a better thing out there. It's just the frustration to get there. So the running, the yoga, the meditation, the AA meetings, the diet, the exercise—all to get himself better. And I'm learning that today.

Patty, it's gonna be all right. You're always here; your teachings are always with us. You're a good man. We went through a lot and we're still goin' through a lot. You're missed here. You're very missed.

Journal Entry – September 20, 2005

I haven't really studied clouds from an airplane in a very long time. But there is something about the light being cast on the vast white skyscape that alternates bizarrely between a straight-out-of-childhood fantasy vision of Heaven, soft stepping stones to meet the angels, and that of a harsh and frozen vista of Hell. Mesmerized, I stare out the window, and wonder, and feel very small.

There are two nuns in Austria who pray for me. Gloria, my Viennese friend, told me their story. My extremely limited knowledge of nuns can be summed up in a couple of stereotypes, and these two who have me in their prayers make me ponder the smallness of my mind.

On September 11th, 2001, Sister G. went to a neighbor's house for a short visit. The majority of Sisters from her contemplative monastery live like recluses in the hermitage; only two of them provide the link to the exterior world—running errands, cleaning the chapel, selling candles. Sister G. is one of them, along with Sister C.

When she entered the living room, the whole family sat transfixed in front of the television and cried, "Look, please! Look at this!" Sister G. thought it was a science-fiction film. In fact, it was the fall of the North Tower. When she understood that all this was reality, she kept watching for a half-hour, seeing again and again the first scenes of the attack. In this country, it was afternoon; in New York City, between 10:28 and 11:00 a.m.

Sister G., who had not watched TV or seen a film in the last thirty years, was very amazed that, in a way, she had been "connected" to this dramatic and crucial event. She asked herself what God wanted to tell her.

From a friend in Vienna, Sister G. and Sister C. first heard about Patrick Brown, and about the far-reaching influence he had and apparently still has on people's lives. The friend sent some pictures and articles.

In April, 2001, both Sisters got special permission from their Superior to watch Stephen McCarthy's video-tribute to Patrick Brown and were deeply impressed. Both told their friend more than once, over the years, that they are feeling sometimes a special influence, a positive atmosphere—something that is impossible to express in words.

The moment on 9/11 when Sister G. had her first look at TV in so many years, she saw Patrick Brown's death. It might not be too bold to assume that she and Sister C. are feeling something of his continuing presence, in God.

KATHLEEN PEMBLE – wife of Charlie Flood, FDNY (song)

ENGINE 73 (THERE FOR YOU) –

We all know someone
Who knows someone who…
But you may not have one
Who's coming home to you.

There, the fire is still burning,
There, you are still digging through
There, every day you are standing,
Every day you are falling
And you have your brothers
Waiting there for you.

Now every man there is somebody's baby
And someone's tender heart to rest upon
And every man among you held his head up high
Walked into the sky…

E-MAIL TO FRIENDS AND FAMILY

Subject: A DAY IN THE CITY
Date: September 14, 2001

I had to go into the city today; I couldn't just be in this peaceful little town watching the news all day long, calling firehouses for information, feeling useless. I needed to go to the firehouses and talk to people who knew Pat and John and Terry, and be in their work surroundings.

I put on all my fire gear—Harlem Hilton hat and T-shirt, Rescue 2 sweatshirt, Pat's captain's bar pin, and his old lieutenant bars that I had long ago made into earrings (ever the fashionista). Partly as tribute, but also to get me past the barricades they had set up at 14th Street, and again at Houston Street. The police were only letting people past with ID, people who live there.

On the way, I passed the impromptu tributes—in front of all the firehouses, and the huge one at Union Square. I am sure you have seen it on the news: very personal notes and mementos, poems, psalms, artwork, and photos of people still missing. And, of course, flowers and candles blanketing the sidewalks.

I went wherever my instincts led me—it was very cathartic to go to places with meaning or comfort, or that felt familiar or safe. But eerie not to have the towers in view, and no traffic, and the acrid air filling every breath, and most especially, the almost total absence of people, except at the barricades and tribute sites, where there were throngs.

At every firehouse, I asked if there was any more news (so many rumors were floating around). But there never was.

The guys were incredible—they want to take care of your comfort level, while most of their group is buried in pulverized cement. I got ushered into kitchens, was offered food, and could not leave Ladder 5 without a huge container of zucchini penne and a bag of cookies. I was embarrassed. But it's what they do; it's programmed into them. I didn't know how long I'd be in the city, and I was thankful to have my doggie bag when I finally got my appetite back, near Stuyvesant Town. That is the complex where Pat lives, and a candlelight vigil was going on at dusk in one of the pathway ovals that connect the modest red-brick buildings. I left a bouquet of sunflowers propped against the locked entrance to 319 Avenue C, and quietly walked away.

Finally, it was time for one last stop at Ladder 3 for any update on Pat. A tired, dusty, young firefighter was sitting on the bench in front and started talking to me. He had just done a shift in the debris and was resting before turning around and going right back down. As we were sitting there, anyone who walked by would tell him they loved him and all the firefighters for what they do, and it was really moving to feel all the support that was coming from the average New Yorker. Banners were hung across the street from NYU housing windows with similar messages, and I realized that in the end, people are what get us through times like these. They can be friends or strangers, but there is an energy that is both spiritual and very human. I never set foot in a church, but this "walking meditation" was just what I needed to do today.

Love, Sharon

DAVID MASON – (poem)

A SURVIVOR

A man sits down because his world has burst
and stares into the desert of his hands.
Though powder chokes him, he does not feel thirst.

His mind descends a million flights of stairs.
When suffocation thundered up the street
he couldn't remember any of his prayers.

A stranger touches him. He tries to stand,
but something's missing in his knees. He can't
turn at his waist to take the stranger's hand.

He hears fresh voices rushing under the din
just as he did before the ceiling fell—
the voices of more firemen going in—

and blinks back chalk to read the sweated lines
auguring in palms that he has years to live.
If only he believed these simple signs.

Where did the sparrows and the heroes go
when heaven dropped and rabble went on burning?
He asks ten fingers. None of them seems to know.

What were their names? How did he get away?
Mute fingers gather to a temple door.
Tomorrow he'll remember how to pray.

I wrote this poem in honor of New York Fire Captain Patrick Brown,
who was killed in the collapse of the north WTC tower, along with eleven

other members of Ladder Company 3. Captain Brown, one of the most decorated firemen in the city, was legendary for his courage. A Vietnam veteran and yoga student, Brown was known as a quiet and much-loved man who had led an immensely colorful life.

"The hero is one who kindles a great light in the world, who sets up blazing torches in the dark streets of life for men to see by."

——Felix Adler

Journal Entry – May 14, 2005

In almost four years now, I have neither asked nor sought to find out exactly where Pat was when his tower fell. This statistical information—a floor number, basically—would then take on a personal weight so heavy it would never again be a simple double digit. I know, because of what I do with the number 343. It could be a digital clock face, a street address, a page in a book. A glance at that symmetrical sequence automatically tallies the lost of NY's Bravest that day. Three hundred forty-three is now a default setting in my psyche.

So here I am, finally needing to know. Is it simply a literary device to bring this project to a fitting end? Or is it an act of almost unbearable intimacy—trying to recreate as best I can Pat's last moments of earthly existence?

DISPATCHER'S TRANSCRIPT – September 11, 2001, 8:47 a.m.

Ladder 3: Three Truck to Manhattan.

Dispatcher: Three Truck.

Ladder 3: Civilian reports from up here, a plane just crashed into the World Trade Center for your information.

Dispatcher: 10-4 K.

Ladder 3: Three Truck's available.

DON HAYDE – Battalion Chief, FDNY

I could feel the hairs go up on the back of my neck—I could hear Patty on the radio. He hadn't been assigned yet to the WTC; he kept trying to get assigned. I don't know where they (3 Truck) were, but after trying two or three times, he came back and tells the dispatcher that they just received a verbal alarm from a civilian about the Trade Tower. Once you receive notification from somebody you have to take action. So the dispatcher had to acquiesce.

PAT BROWN

"Captain Pat Brown, Ladder 3. Captain Pat Brown, Ladder 3. Forty-fourth floor. Exit is proceeding orderly."

PETE CRITSIMILIOS – FDNY

Pat Brown, one of the most decorated men in the history of our department, was on the upper floors when he gave his last radio transmission. "This is Captain Pat Brown, Ladder 3. Evacuation is going smoothly." He was cool, calm, collected.

GREGG HANSSON – Lieutenant, Engine 24

We heard Captain Pat Brown from Ladder 3 giving a message about a collapse in the sixties.

Congressional Record House Presentation of Public Safety Officer Medal of Valor:

By honoring those who died, we also honor those who live on and embody the spirit of those who paid the ultimate sacrifice for the well-being of others. Over the coming years, we will hear tremendous stories of heroic measures. One such story I have heard already is that of Captain

Patrick Brown of 3 Truck on 13th Street in Manhattan. My cousin Michael, whose brother John was killed on that fateful day, works in 3 Truck and was a close friend to Pat and 11 of the members of that fire-fighter unit that were lost that day.

He told me of a radio message that day from the 32nd floor of Tower One…that Pat and other members of 3 Truck were with about forty injured people on their way down from the building. Pat Brown was one of the most decorated members of the FDNY, and when he spoke, every-one listened. A few moments after giving his location in the tower, he radioed again, except this time it was a mayday call, and that the walls of the building were buckling. This was a full ten minutes before the building actually collapsed. It gave firefighters and unknown numbers of rescue workers and victims time to evacuate the building.

Pat Brown and the other men of 3 Truck were in impeccable condition and could easily have gotten out of the building, but Pat Brown called back on his radio that he would be staying behind, that he and the other members from 3 Truck would be staying behind with the injured victims, knowing that they, too, would meet the same fate. If that is not heroism, I do not know what is.

THOMAS VON ESSEN — Excerpt from *Strong Of Heart*

Among the missing was Captain Patrick "Patty" Brown of Ladder 3. One of our toughest firefighters, he also had been one of our most colorful characters: an active bachelor, Vietnam War veteran, yoga enthusiast, often-decorated firefighter, and absolute maniac who loved every new piece of equipment and backed every step we took toward improving safety. Within a few days of the attacks, we were hearing stories about even after the order to evacuate the north tower was issued, Patty had been taking his troops up the stairs because he heard a mayday from Rescue 1 and needed to respond. He was, simply, a warrior.

TOM O'KANE – Pat's Childhood Friend

I heard he was goin' for Hatton. But, who knows? I would suspect, knowin' Patty, he got pretty high up, and it didn't matter why. He was tryin' to get up there. My bet would be he was probably one of the highest.

SAM CASPERSEN – 9/11 Commission Report Staff Member

E-mail

Subject: RE Pat Brown

Date: June 16, 2005

We believe it was Engine 6 which was on the 54th floor with the NYPD personnel. I would have to caution you not to read too much into reported radio communications. I believe there were some radio communications between firefighters in the North Tower and the South Tower, though they were supposed to be on separate channels. Due to the fact that elevators in the South Tower worked up to the 44th Floor, firefighters there did make it much higher—all the way to the 78.5th floor. It's possible that a firefighter reported of partially collapsed floors in the South Tower—without specifying it as the South Tower, and then Captain Brown heard that, believed it referred to the North Tower and repeated it on the radio.

However, it is also possible that Captain Brown kept climbing after the South Tower collapsed, either because he didn't know it had collapsed, as was the case for many of the firefighters in the North Tower at that time, or because he knew it, but was so brave he still thought he needed to continue climbing the stairs to try to rescue civilians. Under that scenario, it is possible he reached the lower sixties and made a radio communication to that effect.

So, I am sorry to say that you are not likely to ever have a definitive answer as to where Captain Brown was and what he was doing when the North Tower collapsed.

But what is clear is that he showed incredible bravery and acted in a manner which brought—and continues to bring—honor to his family and to the United States of America. The terrorists had two goals: to kill as many Americans as possible and to defeat the American spirit. The bravery shown by

Captain Brown and others proved that the terrorists totally failed in this second goal.

On a personal note, my brother's fiancée died on September 11 as well. She was on the 93rd floor of the North Tower. Captain Brown in effect was trying to rescue her.

JOHN WALSH – Host of *America's Most Wanted*
January 30, 2006
Dear Sharon,

All of us have memories seared into our hearts forever of the unfathomable loss of innocent lives on September 11th. It was a day we saw the worst of mankind and the best of mankind. I like to think our best instincts and actions are what saved us as a nation that day... and when I think of the best of the best, I think of Pat Brown.

Pat was a guy whose job it was to protect lives every single day. It was his job to head toward danger when others would run from it. But I still cannot imagine the guts it must have taken to go into those towers after the planes hit. He went into the unknown, into a situation that no other disaster could have prepared him for.

I remember Pat telling me that fear was always in the back of his mind, but he didn't face it until later on, when he thought about what could have happened. I hope knowing this about him makes it easier to imagine his last moments, moments I believe were free of fear. I believe that in all his years of saving lives, he died just trying to save one more.

You have my deepest sympathy in your loss. I hope you know that Pat lives in my heart as a symbol of unselfish heroism. He was a good, brave man who knew danger, but faced it every day. His actions honor all firefighters, and raise their esteem in the communities they protect.

Pat Brown made a difference.
Sincerely,
John Walsh
Host, America's Most Wanted

CAPTAIN PATRICK J. BROWN – Tape released August 16, 2006

I'm on the 35th floor, okay, okay? Just relay to the command post we're trying to get up. There's numerous civilians at all stairwells, numerous burn injuries are coming down. I'm trying to send them down first. Apparently it's above the 75th floor. I don't know if they got there yet. Okay, Three Truck and we are still heading up. Okay? Thank you.

"When one encounters a hero like Paddy, one does not want to let go."

—HARRY GUSTAFSON

MARK HEFFRON – Contributor to AmericanMemorials.com Tribute Site (song)

WHAT THE FLAG MEANS
Patrick Brown was a Queens fireman.
He captained Ladder Number 3.
He knew the look of the frightened face
That sought the light of liberty.
That day his crew climbed the North Tower stairs
And all our hopes came crashing down,
There he saw that shining face
He'd spent his whole life trying to save.
You know your job is done when your rescue comes
And your life shines like the sun.

I found out about Pat by reading a book checked out of the Central Library in Milwaukee. It described the heroism of the firefighters on 9/11. Like a lot of people, I felt the urge to do something as a tribute to the heroes of 9/11, and when I read about Pat and his life, I made him the main character of the song. There are few people who face the hardships that he did and come out of them with a dedication to make the world a better place. He is a hero in the truest sense. It was Pat I was thinking of when I wrote:

Tonight a storm veils a poor widowed world.

Her lonely tears fall just like the rain.

A young man wakes from a troubled dream

And hears a hero call his name.

And as he makes that fateful vow

He knows his life is not his own.

And a new hope lights the starry sea

High above the Land of Liberty.

JUNE M.K. GUSTAFSON – Middle School Teacher, Hingham, Massachusetts

In 2004 I was working as an inclusion assistant at my town's middle school, desperately desiring my own classroom. At the end of my lesson planning periods, I searched the Internet, wondering how to teach about 9/11. Three years before, we had been saying "never forget." Now people just wanted life to be normal.

The deaths of the firefighters had struck me the hardest, and still stuck with me. I couldn't even imagine the ocean of uniforms that had flooded the streets in the months after 9/11; with the mournful wail of bagpipes, it must have been like a high tide of tears that could not recede until it took all the sadness with it. Some days it was too overwhelming to think about. Maybe I shouldn't teach about that day. Yet something nagged at me—*Where is the good?*

Then it dawned on me. In order to teach about September 11th, I had to teach about the firefighters. But where was the lesson's hook? How to draw them in? What could it be about the firefighters that would make even the most jaded, distracted, bored student want to pay attention, to listen, try to understand, and want to remember? The lesson could demonstrate that those black clouds of smoke and evil intent had silver linings—heroes, and their stories that need to be told.

I started by reading about the firefighters. Every day, I would spend the last five or ten minutes of planning time rereading the *New York Times* "Portraits of Grief" series. These short vignettes provided a glimpse, an essence, of these extraordinary yet ordinary men. The one that caught my eye was the one that read: "Captain Patrick J. Brown—New York's Bravest and Grumpiest." I bookmarked the page and kept reading on. About once a week, I would return to him. The look on Pat's face reminded me of the way sixth and seventh graders will stretch their arms way up in the air, as they plead with you: "Pick me! Pick me!" After a month or so, I could not find any other firefighter with such a varied set of spirits in one soul. Captain Brown became the face of our lesson.

The plan started with a scant, short four pages, ready in spring of 2004. Despite such little information on Captain Brown, the title of his "Portrait of Grief" made an impact on my student, Steve D. This guy hated writing, but somehow he related to what was going on. He liked the idea of writing his own biographical sketch and worked so hard to make it great. I will never forget the title of his piece: "Playing Football, He is Poetry in Motion." It was his best writing for the year. I had to know; what was it about the lesson that compelled him? His response: "I like the way you set us up, Mrs. G. You gave us some real good sketches about one guy and they made him sound so, so…you know, like someone worth remembering…I wanted to have me come across like that…someone worth remembering…through good writing."

I spent that summer delving more into the world of Captain Brown. The lesson has grown ten times its original size, to nearly forty pages. A summer later it was added to, revised, and presented for a post-masters' degree class. Pat and I both got an "A." Yes, some of it is the lesson goals, methods, outcomes, and Massachusetts Curriculum Frameworks Standards. But mostly it is Captain Patrick J. Brown.

In my own classroom, my students relate to Pat in many different ways. If they receive a Hingham Middle School Act of Honor, they come to me proudly holding their certificate and free ice cream coupon, saying: "Hey, I did a 'Paddy Brown!'" Students that I had two years ago will come in and talk about Pat like he is there, or ask about my Captain Brown lesson for the current year. Some continue to mention him in their writing, or feature him in a special project. And well past the 9/11 time frame, students (who tend to forget what happened the day before) brainstorm about heroes in other classes, and Pat's name comes up nearly unanimously. When Dylan K. showed me his hero card of Paddy, tears welled in my eyes and I had to leave the class. Pat made his mark while living, but here he is touching the lives of children he never knew.

Each August before I start the school year, I take out a photo collage of Pat that I assembled for my first year of teaching. After my second year, I had it laminated to stand the test of time. Now, when I pull the collage out of its storage spot, I am in a moment of reunion. He is like an old friend who has spent the summer away. Pat's big reassuring grin reminds me that even I can have courage—the courage to teach, to open up my heart to even the most difficult of students and situations, to live every day as if the next I could be hit by a bus. It's just the bare classroom, with me and Pat, pausing to take in the potential and possibilities. It's a rather exhilarating feeling on a cool late August morning—a gentle breeze in the woods outside whispers to us, September is coming, and it's going to be good.

Pat helped me answer the question: *Where is the good?* It's here, it's now. It's finding what's important now. It's about taking risks. It's about giving wider latitude for errors that most kids in middle school need, but most importantly, it is giving selflessly of oneself to try and treasure every moment of sixth grade and beyond.

HARRY GUSTAFSON – student in Mrs. Winter's English Class, Boston College High School – March, 2006 (excerpt from "Heroes" essay)
A hero does not have to have superpowers, but just be willing to take a risk so that someone else may benefit. A hero must be brave because in

order to make the sacrifice, (he) must be willing to give up the thing that will be lost.

Paddy Brown is a perfect example of a hero.

Journal Entry – July 4, 2005

According to the current "Style" section of *The New York Times*, it is now totally passé to wear that post-9/11 American flag-lapel pin. It's out of style, and we've moved on. The verb "to move" implies action, and "passé" is literally French for what we have moved past.

My own definition of movement involves equilibrium rather than time or distance. Remembrance of what once was ebbs and flows with what now is. It wasn't always so.

When I was younger, I used to walk through the moving subway cars to get to the closest street exit. I challenged myself to not hold on to any bars or strap handles, and to trust my own agility, balance, and sense of anticipation. I got good at it—I rarely lurched. Pat, having nothing to prove to himself about risk-taking, was never impressed with my daring. And he held on to the pole.

To move across town on foot without stopping for a light was another game, involving the art of jaywalking and impeccable timing. Passing riders to walk up escalators, mentally dividing errands by neighborhood—speed and complexity and city life were so tightly intwined into my hard drive that they were virtually inseparable. I thought I would love living at that pace forever.

Things have changed. Movement now evolves out of a stance I take with the world. It is a metaphorical "sanchin," or three-pointed stance that I learned in karate. I plant my feet, knees slightly bent. I concentrate on my *hara*, my center of gravity as well as my spiritual center. I breathe. I absorb. I endure.

Miss you, Pat. We all do.

AUTHOR UNKNOWN – (poem found on Legacy.com Tribute Site)

Couldn't save all the grunts in Nam
But oh how he tried.

Then he gave them his sleeping dreams.

Couldn't save all the damsels in distress
But oh how he tried.

Then he gave them his sleeping dreams.

Couldn't save all the lifers on the park bench
But oh how he tried.

Then he gave them his sleeping dreams.

Couldn't save all the children in the fire
But oh how he tried.

Then he gave them his sleeping dreams.

Couldn't save all the people in the towers
But oh how he tried.

Couldn't save them all
But oh how he tried.

Couldn't save them all
But oh how he tried.

Sleep in peace, Patty Brown
'Cause oh how you tried.

ACKNOWLEDGMENTS

When I embarked upon this project it was with an idealism that only can accompany sincerity of intent and downright naiveté. How could doors NOT fly open? After all, this is Patty Brown we're talking about. The stories were out there. The experience of collecting them often forced me past the confines of my comfort zone, and has both toughened and softened me. For that nudge to my back—thanks, Pat.

This book would not exist without the generous spoken and written contributions shared in these pages by so many people who knew and loved Pat. I am indebted to them for their memories and their trust. My thanks also to Mike and Janet Brown, and Carolyn Brown Negron, for their faith, their warmth, and their sharing of family photos.

Along the journey I've been helped in various ways by the following people: Jim Cypher, Marv Dembinsky, Elizabeth Power, Ellin Martens, James Malcolm, Olinda Cedeno, John Leonard, Margaret Mannion, Amy Green, Terry Quinn, Robin Read, and Nanette Norcia. The FDNY Library's Chief Lerch and Lieutenant Grasso were helpful with my research there.

Barbara Marcus, whose own endeavor (The Face of Courage) is shared in this collection, let me know that a total novice can accomplish her goal, one step at a time, if her heart is in it. Barbara died shortly after sending me her essay, far too young. She made an impact.

Aaron Arehart inadvertently summarized the running theme of my project with his assessment of Pat, a man he never met: "Pat is my hero not because he was lost in the line of duty on September 11, but because of how he lived prior to that day. Learning about Pat, two things struck me most—inspiration and pain. The pain is a hollow feeling that accompanies deep sorrow. It is lessened by Pat's inspiration."

I am indebted to Joan Schweighardt of GreyCore Press for her belief in my project, as well as her untiring practical help in maneuvering through the world of publishing, to Susan Malone for her graceful editing and support, and to Kathleen Massaro, for her intuitive book design and patient calm. You all have made the "birthing process" memorable and remarkable.

And finally, thanks to my support system, my emotional safety net, of family and friends. You all know who you are. Love you.

PROCEEDS OF BOOK SALES will go to Bent On Learning, a not-for-profit program that brings yoga and meditation to NYC public schools and youth centers. For more information go to www.bentonlearning.org.

Credits and grateful acknowledgements for reuse of originally published material:

Made in the USA
Middletown, DE
05 June 2019